SANDWICH CUISINE
Oregon Style

Sandwich Cuisine Oregon Style

JAN ROBERTS-DOMINGUEZ
with illustrations by the author

Drift Creek Press
Philomath, Oregon

A NOTE ON THE PAPER AND BINDING:

SANDWICH CUISINE, Oregon Style has been printed on acid free paper made of recycled fiber. Its pages will not show the yellow of age, common to other papers. The binding has been specifically chosen for the kind of use a cook book receives. The Otabind® method will allow this book to open flat from the first page to the last.

Published by Drift Creek Press
1807 Main Street, PO Box 511, Philomath, Oregon 97370

Library of Congress Cataloging–in–Publication Data
Roberts–Dominguez, Jan.   Sandwich Cuisine: Oregon Style
Jan Roberts–Dominguez
p.188.   8.5 in. x 10 in.   Illustrated.   Includes index
1. Sandwiches   I. Title
TX818.   1990   90-082414
641.8   CIP

ISBN 0-9626441-0-2

Printed and bound in the United States of America
Set in ITC Berkeley Oldstyle
Designed by John Bennett

To my editor, friend, and husband, Steve Dominguez, for his committment, guidance, and ability to hold onto —and build upon—the vision of the project as it first appeared in my mind's eye.

It's done and we're still laughing. What could be better?

Contents

Acknowledgements

Special thanks to my parents, Margaret and Will Roberts, for their encouragement, research and steady flow of good ideas. Also, to Sue Roberts, for recipe research above and beyond the call of most sisters-in-law.

In its early stage, my Oregon Heroes chapter took on a life of its own. There were volumes of biographical information to be obtained, release forms to be signed, and an endless list of details that needed to be incorporated into the chapter. Thanks to the following people and organizations for their assistance: M. Eloise Booker; Mrs. Angus Bowmer; Julia Brim-Edwards; Lisa Cavelier; the Corvallis *Gazette-Times*; Ron Crawford; Marion Cunningham; the Salem *Statesman Journal* Sports Editor Roy Gault; Peter Kump and Caroline Stuart of The James Beard Foundation; the Oregon State University Sports Information Department; Sandi Serling; Ray Steinfeld, Jr.; Brad Teel; Lorraine Ten Pas.

For general inspiration and gracious sharing of their recipes, thanks to Sheri Albin, Debbie and John Griesmeyer, Timberline Lodge Executive Chef Leif Erik Benson, and The Ark Co-owner/Chef Nanci Main.

Thanks to Kay Ochs for becoming my Southern Oregon liaison, to Charlie Hilke for his professional guidance, to Lorinda Moholt of the Oregon Dairy Council for recipes and research, to Lincoln County Extension Agent Bob Jacobson, for sharing everything you'd want to know about Pacific shrimp, and to Annette Forrer for indexing.

Special thanks to my publisher, Craig Battrick, who came to me with the conviction that the world needed one more sandwich cookbook, and believed I was the one to write it.

And finally, to my sons, Brandon and Ryan, special thanks for your support and taste-testing skills. I wish I could promise that the next project will be CHOCOLATE or PIE or COOKIES, but don't hold your breath.

J.R.D.

SANDWICH CUISINE
Oregon Style

Chapter 1

Harvest Celebration

Oregon is very much about beauty. A part of it is the scenery, of course, from snowy peaks astride the mountain ranges, to lush green forests and glens spilling down highland slopes into river valleys, to the expansive grandeur of the high desert, where distance used to be measured in "looks" instead of miles. In the west, the restless Pacific surf grooms long white beaches, or explodes in brilliant fountains against rocky headlands. In the east, the mighty Snake River carves away at awesome Hell's Canyon, having already gouged it deeper than the Grand Canyon of the Colorado. In between, countless rivers and streams murmur their ancient music. And then there are the people, with a kind and generous nature as captivating as all that scenery. One never tires of this setting.

It reminds me of the time I lived and worked in another beautiful place, Yosemite National Park. There the view from my back porch was the full-sized original of what millions of park visitors spend 35 cents plus postage to send back home. Day in and day out I pedaled my bike through that enchanted landscape, past flourishing groves of dogwood, pine and oak set against 2,000-foot granite cliffs draped with foaming ribbons of water.

One afternoon a hotel guest dropped by my desk in the lobby to report on the success of his day's hike. It was great, he said. Magnificent, in fact. But then he thought for a moment, and added: "You know, as beautiful as Yosemite is, I'll bet that when you've lived here for a while, the scenery has as much impact as a painting over your couch. Don't you sometimes forget to appreciate it?"

Well, I didn't know what a "while" was, I told the gentleman. But I knew 25-year park veterans who were still as dumbstruck as I at the surreal pink alpenglow cast from the face of Half Dome at dusk, and old-timers who still teared up at the sight of morning mist rising off the Merced river as it glided through an emerald meadow.

Bored with such everyday stuff as that? Not them. Not me. Not in Yosemite. Not in Oregon.

Among the foremost of Oregon's charms is the prodigious variety of its landscapes. Just about every type of wilderness one could ask for is available somewhere in the state, and the same can be said for lands that have been tamed. Uncounted combinations of climate, topography, and geology make possible an Oregon harvest that is nothing less than a non-stop cornucopia. Where should one begin in portraying such abundance? Where should one end?

The answer comes at 1500 feet over the most splendid

strip of country in the Northwest, the Columbia River Gorge. You gawk, and you ooh, and you ahh. And even though it's February and your stomach is doing triple rollers because a winter storm is surging all around you, when the pilot turns to say, "There's Multnomah Falls," you look. The mountains this river has breached aren't called the Cascades for nothing. Flying on, the storm's mists obscure much of man's handiwork, putting it in perspective among the mightier forces that shape Oregon's living mantle.

From its dramatic sweep into northeast Oregon's dry-land wheat country, to the cattle ranches, orchards, and farms along its gorge and lower reaches, to its gentle oblivion in the rich Pacific Ocean, the Columbia River cuts a cross-section through Oregon's harvest that is as representative as any I can imagine.

I will begin with the ocean.

OREGON PACIFIC SHRIMP

As the 90-foot trawler slices through crested waves, a bank of wheeling, squawking gulls hangs overhead. The net has just been brought aboard after an hour's drag through the chill waters off the Oregon coast, and half a ton of tiny Pacific shrimp, as well as a tangle of rockfish, sole, smelt, hake, anchovy and sea urchins, tumble out into the sorting hopper. Wind pounces on the fishermen as they quickly reset the net for another drag, a process that's repeated up to ten times a day.

Commercial fishing is never a cakewalk. But at least shrimpers work during the more civilized seasons of early spring through mid-autumn. When the weather's good they'll stay out up to four days, stowing their catch on ice.

The real problem is that the annual harvest varies on a roller-coaster ten year cycle, from as much as 57 million pounds to as little as 4 million. Reasons for the fluctuation remain unclear, but they are not thought to include overfishing.

The largest shrimp ground lies between the Columbia River and Yaquina Head. Hence, the ports of Astoria and Newport process the most shrimp. The biggest loads arrive in early April, just when the season gets under way.

Of course, it follows that this is the best time for Oregon shrimp lovers to make like seagulls and flock to the nearest wharf. That first shrimp cocktail of the season tastes mighty good. Especially when eaten along the wharf, where the shrimp are freshest and the saltwater tang in the air enhances their delicate-sweet essence.

Eventually, though, you'll want an alternative to the trusty shrimp cocktail. That's the time to try the sandwich approach.

Oregon Shrimp with Tomato & Guacamole

*OREGON SHRIMP WITH TOMATO
    & GUACAMOLE*

*2 slices sour dough French bread,
    toasted*

Mayonnaise

2 slices tomato

1/3 cup fresh Oregon Pacific shrimp

*1/2 teaspoon fresh snipped dill
    (or 1/4 teaspoon dried)*

*Generous dollop of guacamole
    (page 169)*

Spread each slice of toasted bread with a small amount of mayonnaise. Top one slice with the tomatoes, a sprinkling of dill, the shrimp and a dollop of guacamole. Place second slice of bread on top. Yields 1 serving.

SPRING SALMON

From a culinary point of view, ocean-caught spring salmon are the most prized. At this phase of their life cycle, maximal body fat makes them their most tender and flavorful.

Of the five species of Pacific salmon, chinook, also known as king salmon, is considered premier. It has the most body fat—up to 16 percent. At the other end of the scale is the pink, or humpback salmon, with a fat content rarely exceeding 4 percent.

The coho, also called the silver salmon, is less oily than the chinook, but is still considered a flavorful catch. So is the sockeye or red salmon, although for years it rarely made it to the fresh market because canners appreciated its attractive red flesh.

One of the finest ways to prepare spring chinook is to barbecue it over natural mesquite charcoal. Broiling, poaching in white wine, and pan-frying are certainly worthy approaches too.

Or, you could try this wonderful coulibiac.

Columbia River Salmon Coulibiac

This is a sandwich, of sorts, being a savory strudel-like concoction of puff pastry wrapped around a delicate salmon filling. It was created by Leif Eric Benson, Executive Chef at Timberline Lodge for his cookbook, *Timberline Lodge Cookbook—Northwest Seasonal Recipes*.

COLUMBIA RIVER SALMON
   COULIBIAC

1 pound fresh salmon fillet, 3/4 to
   1 inch thick

1 medium onion, chopped

1 tablespoon butter

1 pound fresh spinach, washed, chopped,
   and cooked

1 hard-cooked egg

3/4 cup white fish, such as cod, sole, or
   snapper, cooked and broken into
   small pieces

1 cup cooked wild rice

1/2 cup Béchamel Sauce
   (recipe follows)

1 tablespoon chopped fresh dill
   (or 2 teaspoons dried)

1 tablespoon thyme

Zest of 1 lemon

Salt and white pepper to taste

1 sheet frozen puff pastry, thawed

Egg wash: 1 egg, 1 tablespoon water

1 cup Hollandaise Sauce (recipe follows)

Skin the salmon and remove any bones. Set aside. Sauté the onion in the butter until translucent. Combine the spinach, hard-cooked egg, white fish, sautéed onion, wild rice, Béchamel Sauce, dill, thyme, and lemon zest. Mix lightly and season to taste with the salt and pepper. Set aside.

Roll out the puff pastry sheet so that it is 2 inches longer than twice the length of the salmon fillet, and 1-1/2 to 2 inches wider than the fillet. At this point, the pastry should be about 1/8 inch thick. If it is thicker, continue rolling until it is the proper thickness.

Spread a layer of the spinach mixture in the middle of the pastry. Place the salmon fillet on the spinach and then spread another layer of the spinach mixture over the salmon. Beat the egg and water together to form a wash. Fold the pastry over the filling and seal it with the egg wash. Turn it over so that the seam side is down.

Place on a greased cookie sheet and bake in a 350° oven for 30 to 45 minutes, or until brown. The internal temperature of the salmon should be 130° when done. It can be tested with a meat thermometer.

Note: When using frozen puff pastry, be sure to defrost it overnight in the refrigerator, and keep it refrigerated until it is used. When baked, this dough separates and "puffs" into a myriad of delicate pastry layers.

To serve, slice crosswise into 1-inch thick sections and serve with Hollandaise Sauce. Yields 4 servings.

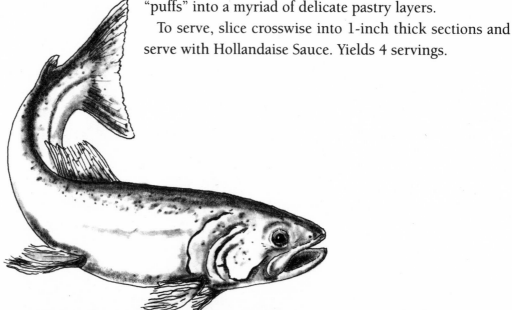

In a saucepan, sauté the onion in the butter until the onion is translucent. Stir in the flour. Cook a few minutes, or until it becomes bubbly and foamy. Gradually add the milk, whisking slowly. Bring to a boil, add the seasonings, and allow to simmer for 30 minutes, stirring occasionally to prevent burning. Strain the sauce through a fine sieve and use. Yields 3 cups.

BECHAMEL SAUCE

1/4 medium onion, minced

2 tablespoons butter

4 tablespoons flour

3 cups milk

1/4 teaspoon salt

3 whole peppercorns

1 sprig parsley

Pinch of nutmeg

1 whole clove

Assemble all the ingredients and read the instructions carefully before beginning. The preparation of this sauce requires concentration and speed.

Combine the white wine, lemon juice, salt, and peppers in a saucepan, bring to a boil, and reduce over very high heat until half the liquid has evaporated. Remove the saucepan from the heat and let it cool for a few minutes.

Add the egg yolks one at a time, beating constantly with a wire whisk. Put the saucepan back on very low heat (or over a pan of very hot water, double boiler fashion). Heat the sauce again, beating it constantly. When it becomes creamy, remove it from the heat and let it cool while continuing to beat it gently. When the sauce is just cool enough to touch, begin adding the clarified butter, which should be at the same temperature as the sauce, very gradually. The first addition should be just a few drops. Beat the mixture well after each addition and add a larger quantity of butter each time. It is very important to fully incorporate each addition of butter before adding more. When the butter is fully combined, strain the mixture through a fine sieve. Serve warm. Yields 3-1/2 cups.

HOLLANDAISE SAUCE

1/4 cup dry white wine

Juice of 1 lemon

1 teaspoon salt

Pinch of white pepper

Pinch of cayenne pepper

4 egg yolks

3 cups clarified butter

Source: *Timberline Lodge Cookbook, Northwest Seasonal Recipes,* by Leif Eric Benson, Graphic Arts Center Publishing Co.

DUNGENESS CRAB

There are so many gastronomical benefits to Oregon living that I suppose giving up one or two wouldn't matter—as long as one of them wasn't Dungeness crab. Even without the accouterments of an all-out crab feast—the crowd, wine, crunchy sourdough French bread, a big green salad and zesty Louis dressing—Dungeness crab would still be terrific.

For size, Dungeness falls between its East Coast cousin, the blue crab, and the West Coast Alaskan king crab. On the average, the Dungeness weighs in from 1-3/4 to 3-1/2 pounds, whereas its Alaskan buddy can come as large as 20 pounds, with a leg span of nearly 6 feet. The genteel blue crab rarely grows larger than a pound. Although in the middle size-wise, I believe Dungeness is the hands down winner for flavor and texture. Only during its molting season, from August through October, is the Dungeness less than perfect. After shedding its shell, it absorbs large amounts of water, which makes it less tasty.

About the only downside for Dungeness crab aficionados is the unpredictable pricing from year to year. When the crab population goes down, and it does fluctuate, prices go up.

But for my family, live crab has always been worth the expense. Even my brother, an unlikely contestant for Spendthrift of the Year, springs for crab dinners when his sister hits town. There are few better spots to catch up on family affairs than in the kitchen, over a bubbling crab pot.

Dungeness Crab in Lemon & Herb Sauce

The subtle, lemony character of the homemade mayonnaise is the perfect foil for the delicate flavor of fresh Dungeness crab. Equally delicate shallots are the onions of choice.

In a large bowl, combine crab, celery and shallots. Toss well to blend ingredients. Gently fold in the Lemon & Herb Sauce, adding more as needed, to reach desired consistency.

Place the slices of bread on a baking sheet and broil until golden; remove from oven. Spread the toasted side of each slice with a portion of the crab mixture, then return to oven and broil just until tops are golden. Yields 8 sandwiches.

In a blender or food processor, combine the egg, wine vinegar, lemon juice, mustard, lemon peel, sugar, salt, tarragon and paprika. Blend the mixture for a few seconds. With the motor running, slowly add the salad oil—drop by drop at first until mixture thickens, then in a slow, steady stream. The mixture will have the consistency of a soft mayonnaise. Yields about 1-1/4 cups.

DUNGENESS CRAB IN
  LEMON & HERB SAUCE

1 pound fresh Dungeness crab meat
  (about 3 1/2 cups)
1/2 cup finely minced celery
1/4 cup finely minced shallots
About 1/2 to 3/4 cup Lemon & Herb
  Sauce (recipe follows)
8 slices sourdough French bread
  (cut 1/2-inch thick)

LEMON & HERB SAUCE

1 egg
1-1/2 tablespoons red or white wine
  vinegar
1-1/2 tablespoons lemon juice
2 teaspoons Dijon-style mustard
1-1/2 teaspoons grated lemon peel
1 teaspoon sugar
1/2 teaspoon salt
1/2 teaspoon minced fresh tarragon
  (or 1/4 teaspoon dried)
1/4 teaspoon paprika
1 cup salad oil

ALBACORE

Millions of tuna/mayo sandwiches in little brown bags notwithstanding, this tired rendition of tuna cuisine hardly sparks the taste buds. I mean, when was the last time you salivated over such fare at a dinner party?

But fresh albacore tuna from the meat case? Now there's an intriguing thought. From trawler to grill to plate, with no salty layover in one of those little flat cans—that's the ticket. Through summer and into fall, schools of these beautiful silvery-black fish abound only a few hundred miles off the Oregon coast, as they migrate north. Their timing couldn't be better for outdoor chefs.

Of all the tunas, albacore has the lightest-colored meat and mildest flavor. Its high oil content keeps it from drying out during cooking and its mellow flavor complements a variety of cooking styles.

Grilled Albacore Sandwich with Sautéed Peppers in Sherry & Lemon Dill Sauce

GRILLED ALBACORE SANDWICH WITH SAUTEED PEPPERS IN SHERRY & LEMON DILL SAUCE

1-1/2 pounds skinless Pacific albacore, cut into 3/4-inch thick loin sections

3 tablespoons olive oil

6 tablespoons lemon juice. . .

Place albacore in a shallow dish or re-sealable plastic bag. Combine olive oil, lemon juice, oregano, salt, pepper and cayenne and pour half of it over the fish. Marinate the albacore in this mixture for 30 minutes. Meanwhile, pour enough of the reserved marinade into the sour cream to reach a somewhat thin (but not soupy) consistency. Add dill and lemon zest and set aside. Drain albacore, reserving the marinade for basting fish as it cooks. Place albacore on a greased grill 4 to 5 inches over hot coals and cook about 6 minutes, turning once and basting frequently. Do not overcook. The albacore should be removed while still slightly pink in the center because it will continue to cook while still hot.

If desired, brush inside faces of French rolls with reserved marinade that hasn't contacted the fish, then toast the rolls on the grill.

To assemble the sandwiches, spread bottom half of each roll with some of the sour cream dill sauce, then add a slab of albacore. Top each serving with a portion of the Sautéed Peppers and fresh basil, drizzle on a small amount of the sour cream sauce, add the tops of the buns, and serve. Yields 4 servings.

Heat olive oil in a skillet over medium-high heat. Add mushrooms and onions, then sauté until mushrooms release their juices and the liquid is reduced. Add sherry and Worcestershire sauce and continue to cook until liquid is reduced again. After adding peppers and garlic, cook until the peppers are soft and the mushrooms nicely browned. Remove pan from heat and sprinkle with freshly grated Parmesan cheese.

1/2 teaspoon dried oregano, crushed
1/4 teaspoon salt
1/4 teaspoon white pepper
Generous dash of cayenne
1/2 cup sour cream
1/2 teaspoon dried dill
1/4 teaspoon grated lemon zest
Sautéed Peppers (recipe follows)
4 French rolls, split lengthwise
1/4 cup chopped fresh basil

SAUTEED PEPPERS

2 tablespoons olive oil
1 cup thinly sliced mushrooms
2 onions, sliced into 1/4-inch rings
1/4 cup dry sherry
1/2 teaspoon Worcestershire sauce
1 red and 1 yellow sweet bell pepper,
    sliced into 1/4-inch rings
2 cloves garlic, minced
Freshly grated Parmesan cheese

CANEBERRIES

Summers hit hard in the Willamette Valley when they finally arrive in late July. On sultry evenings after scorcher days, it's good to step outdoors and meander along country roads draped in musty-sweet streamers of fragrance from ripening blackberries. Soon the sunbaked wild canes will yield their bounty to any birds, beasts, or canners willing to brave their prickly tangles. Meanwhile, there are the raspberries. The more cultured fruit in the berry family, the raspberry's velvety exterior and sumptuous flavor go hand in hand with silver service, crystal goblets and fancy tarts. But don't let its reputation mislead you. It's still just another member of the caneberry clan. Just as respectable are the Marionberry—named for the Willamette Valley county where it was developed—Cascadeberry, Boysenberry and Loganberry.

Put any of them to use and the result is the same: wonderful.

Chicken Salad Sandwich in Raspberry Vinaigrette

Combine chicken, cabbage, Swiss cheese, onion and Raspberry Vinaigrette. Add additional vinaigrette to reach desired consistency. Refrigerate mixture for 1 hour to blend flavors.

To assemble sandwiches, spread bottom half of each roll with mayonnaise. Add portions of the chicken filling, sprinkle with bacon, add a few slices of tomato, and finish with tops of rolls. Yields 4 servings.

CHICKEN SALAD SANDWICH IN RASPBERRY VINAIGRETTE

2 cups diced cooked breast of chicken

1 cup shredded red cabbage

1 cup shredded Swiss cheese

1/2 cup green onion

1 cup Raspberry Vinaigrette
  (recipe follows)

4 French rolls, split

Mayonnaise

6 slices bacon, cooked and crumbled

Tomato slices

In a small bowl, whisk together raspberry vinegar, raspberry preserves, mustard and honey. Slowly add 1 cup vegetable oil, whisking constantly to blend. Yields about 2 cups.

This is also a wonderful vinaigrette for grapefruit and melon salad, or as a tangy dressing for spinach salad.

RASPBERRY VINAIGRETTE

1/3 cup raspberry vinegar
     (recipe follows, or use commercial
     variety)
1/3 cup raspberry preserves
2 tablespoons Dijon mustard
1 tablespoon honey
1 cup vegetable oil

Raspberry vinegar is available commercially, but it's simple to make. Here's how. Simmer vinegar, sugar and raspberries together for 10 minutes. Cool, then cover and steep for 2 or 3 days in a cool spot. Pour the steeped mixture through several layers of cheesecloth into a clean jar with a tight-fitting lid. Yields about 2 cups.

RASPBERRY VINEGAR

2 cups white wine vinegar
2 tablespoons sugar
1 cup fresh raspberries

STRAWBERRIES

There are those who endure the downside of a soggy Northwest spring only because they know the pot at the end of the rainbow is filled with sweet, juicy, Oregon strawberries.

James Beard knew about Oregon berries. He talked often of the wild strawberries that grew along the coast near his boyhood town of Gearhart. They were so small that it took hours to gather enough to satisfy one's appetite. But they were so good that no one minded. He said they were filled with a sugary, wild essence that lingered on his palate and filled him with a nostalgia that stayed with him even into his later years.

Most Oregonians would echo those thoughts, even for commercial berries. It's a pity the season is so short. The most common varieties you'll encounter these days are the Benton, Hood, Shuksan, Totem and Rainier. Opinions on which is "the best" vary. Generally, the Benton and Hood are considered ideal for fresh eating, due to a slightly lower acidity, whereas the other varieties are ideal for cooking and canning.

But while most merely revel in the splendor of fresh Oregon strawberries, food preservers and commercial packers are always casting an eye ahead to less bountiful times. Times when homemade strawberry preserves would be the perfect topping for your morning toast. Times in the deep of winter when you can haul out your precious cache of ruby-fruited jam and bring a smile back into the kitchen.

Woodburn fruit packer Bob Conroy remembers the first major commercial freezing efforts, which began over a half century ago. "We used to pack them in 50 gallon wooden barrels. Then we'd stack them in cold storage areas where those old compressors could actually get the temperature down to about 5 degrees below zero and keep it there."

Conroy said that the hefty barrels containing about 375 pounds of fruit and sugar had to be rolled every two days until the contents were completely frozen. "And oh boy, was that a lot of work. They didn't have lift trucks, so it had to be done by hand."

Packing was also done by hand. The ratio was about 90 pounds of sugar to 285 pounds of fruit, he said. Give or take a few pounds.

"They just sort of layer-packed them. They'd run in about 3 inches of fruit, then about half an inch of sugar.

And then they'd put about 6 inches of fruit and 3 inches of sugar, and so on, until the barrel was filled. It wasn't perfectly accurate, but it was close enough."

Then, in 1938, Birdseye introduced the first retail pack of frozen strawberries. "It was a daring thing to do," he recalled. But the public took to the little packages of fruit that had been packed right there in Hillsboro. "Can you imagine," exclaimed Conroy, "strawberries at Christmas time!"

For Conroy, the memory of standing on the line thirty-three years ago as the berries from Forest Grove came into the plant is still vivid. "I'd take a berry off the line as they were running by and hold it between my forefinger and thumb. Then I would sliiiide it through the sugar to build up a real good coating. Ooooh, that was good."

Strawberries & Cream Cheese Breakfast Muffins

In a bowl, combine granola, apple, hazelnuts, coconut, honey and lemon juice; set aside. Spread the muffin halves first with butter, and then with the cream cheese mixture. Layer on the granola mixture, and then arrange the sliced berries on top. Yields 2 open-face sandwiches; 1 or 2 servings.

STRAWBERRIES & CREAM CHEESE
  BREAKFAST MUFFINS

1/4 cup granola

1 apple, peeled, cored and chopped

1/3 cup coarsely chopped toasted hazelnuts

1 tablespoon shredded or flaked coconut

1 tablespoon honey

2 teaspoons fresh lemon juice

1 raisin English muffin, toasted and cooled

Softened butter or margarine

2 tablespoons each (combine): softened
  cream cheese, plain yogurt

6 fresh Oregon strawberries, hulled and
  sliced

LEEKS

At a time of year when most vegetables are but a twinkle in the farmer's eye, or are nestled in greenhouses await-ing spring, the leek is toughing out the winter in not-so-cozy Northwest fields.

Oregon leeks, planted in late May, take three months to develop. Once they've reached maturity, they store nicely right where they are—in the ground. Growers harvest the crop only as needed, until the plants go to seed the following May.

Before using leeks in a recipe you have to deal with the soil collected under their broad, flat leaves. Begin by removing any withered outer leaves, then cut off and dis-card the upper green leaves down to the point where the dark green begins to pale. Halve each leek lengthwise to within 1-1/2 inches of its base, gently fan out its remain-ing leaves, and plunge it into a sinkful of water several times to rinse the grit away.

The following sandwich is adapted from a recipe I cre-ated several years ago: Leeks Braised in Butter and Sherry, Au Gratin, which has brought me fond memories and not a little chagrin. When I demonstrated it on Portland television station KATU's morning talk show, host Jim Bosley made the mistake of praising my flamboyant technique with the sauté pan. Rising to the compliment, I shook and tossed the simmering leeks and cheese ever higher into the air, until they finally arched out of the pan altogether and onto Jim's shiny black dress shoes. Cut to commercial.

Sautéed Leeks with Ham Sandwich

Melt butter in a heavy, ovenproof skillet over medium-high heat. Add leeks and sauté until softened, about 3 minutes. Add sherry, salt and white pepper and continue to cook until leeks are tender, about 5 minutes. Stir in cream and cook a couple of minutes longer to reduce the liquid slightly; remove from heat.

To assemble the sandwiches, spread one side of each bread slice with a little mayonnaise and mustard. Place 6 of the slices on a baking sheet, mayonnaise up. Arrange slices of ham on these bread slices, followed by a layer of the leek mixture. Finish by sprinkling on the Jack and Parmesan cheeses. Broil just until leek mixture is golden. Top each sandwich with second slice of bread and serve. Yields 6 sandwiches.

SAUTEED LEEKS
  WITH HAM SANDWICH

6 tablespoons butter

4 cups chopped leeks (about 5 1-inch
  diameter leeks)

2 tablespoons dry sherry

1/4 teaspoon salt

1/4 teaspoon white pepper

1/3 cup heavy cream

12 slices pumpernickel bread

Mayonnaise

Dijon-style mustard

6 slices ham, 1/4-inch thick

1/2 cup shredded Monterey Jack cheese

1/4 cup grated Parmesan cheese

HAZELNUTS

Three hazelnut trees for every Oregonian. On a per capita basis, that's what Oregon's hazelnut orchards amount to. But it all started over 100 years ago with just a handful of seeds brought to Oregon from France by David Gernot. In no time at all he had 50 trees, and a lot of Oregon farmers began thinking that maybe they could do as well. As it became clear that this was a crop to bank on, more growers followed suit, dedicating acre upon fertile acre to orchards. An industry was born.

Today, 98 percent of the domestic hazelnut crop grows on 25,000 acres of Oregon soil, mostly within the climatically temperate Willamette Valley. Mild winters are vital in order for the hazelnut to sustain its curious sex life. Unlike most other fruiting trees, hazelnuts blossom in January and February. While you and I are inside fumbling with comforters and woolen snuggies, the hazelnut is out there pollinating up a storm.

Several summers ago I drove through an old Willamette Valley orchard with a grower. Although a good 27 feet separated the trunks, the afternoon sun was filtered by a nearly unbroken dusty-green canopy. As we bumped along, gnarled branches sometimes reached low enough to scrap the roof of the truck. It was late August and the grass-green nuts punctuated their dark leafy background like stars. This was when I finally understood the derivation of the hazelnut's alternate name of filbert, or "full beard," because the outer husk sports a leafy fringe that is truly beard-like in appearance.

By late September or October those frilly outer shells have released the ripened nuts. As they lie on the ground ready to be harvested, they sport the yellowish red-brown hue that has become known as "hazel." The name hazel originated from the Anglo-Saxon "haesel," or helmet. This, of course, is the shape of the hazelnut.

Chicken Salad Sandwich with Roasted Hazelnuts

CHICKEN SALAD SANDWICH WITH
ROASTED HAZELNUTS

4 chicken breast halves, cooked, boned
and diced . . .

In a bowl, combine chicken, hazelnuts, celery and water chestnuts. In a small bowl, blend together the mayonnaise, vinegar, onion, soy sauce, curry powder and ginger; stir this combination into the chicken mixture; chill. To serve, stuff each French roll with a portion of the filling. Garnish each sandwich with sliced tomatoes and green sweet bell pepper rings. Yields 4 servings.

1/2 cup chopped toasted hazelnuts

1/2 cup finely chopped celery

1/4 cup chopped water chestnuts

1/2 cup mayonnaise

2 tablespoons wine vinegar

1 tablespoon minced onion

2 teaspoons soy sauce

1/2 teaspoon curry powder

1/2 teaspoon powdered ginger

4 French rolls, split lengthwise

Garnishes: sliced tomatoes, green sweet bell pepper rings

BUNCH ONIONS

By June, bunch onions are at their peak. A bunch onion, for the uninitiated, is the baby version of a mature red or white onion, and looks very much like an over-grown green onion with the lush green stalks still attached. The entire onion, from stalk to orb, is extremely mild and tender, and completely edible.

Focaccia Bread Special with Bunch Onions & Olive Oil

*FOCACCIA BREAD SPECIAL WITH
BUNCH ONIONS & OLIVE OIL*

*2 bunches of bunch onions, thinly sliced,
to measure about 2 or 3 cups of
onions (use entire globe, plus about
two-thirds of the green portion)*

2 cloves garlic, finely minced

1/4 cup olive oil

*1 (14-1/2 ounce) can Italian-style
stewed tomatoes*

Salt and white pepper to taste

1-1/2 cups shredded Cheddar cheese

1/3 cup grated Parmesan cheese

*1 (8- or 9-inch) round of focaccia bread
(these are marketed in a brown 'n
serve form, and are distributed
nationally in most supermarkets.)*

Sauté the onions and garlic in olive oil just until onions are softened, about 2 minutes. Add the stewed tomatoes and simmer until mixture thickens, about 10 minutes. Adjust seasonings with salt and pepper.

Place the loaf of focaccia bread in a lightly greased 9-inch round cake pan. Spread half of the onion mixture on top of the loaf, making sure it gets down into all of the holes on the surface. Sprinkle on half of the Cheddar and Parmesan. Top with remaining onion mixture, then sprinkle with remaining Cheddar and Parmesan.

Bake in 425° oven about 20 or 25 minutes, until top is beautifully browned and bubbly. Remove from oven and let the loaf rest for about 5 minutes before removing from pan and cutting into serving-sized wedges. A delicious meal when served with plainly grilled meats and a big salad. Yields 6 servings.

ADAPTATIONS ABOUND: To the onion mixture, add any number of chopped vegetables as they come into season, such as sweet bell peppers, Walla Walla Sweet onions, and celery. Other delicious toppings include pepperoni, cooked sausage, sliced olives, and mushrooms. Exercise your imagination!

PEACHES

Nobody has to tell you how to enjoy your first summer peach. Ignoring the faint tickling of fuzz against your lips as you bite into the juicy flesh, you simply eat it—out of hand, in four healthy bites. Then, as you wipe the trails of nectar from your chin and throw the pit at whomever's closest, you can contemplate the rest of the season. It's a short one, of course. Peaking in August, and trailing off by late September when the last of the u-pick fields are finally exhausted.

The river valleys—the Rogue, Umpqua and Willamette—as well as the fertile lands of Eastern Oregon, produce this tender crop.

Peaches & Cream Cheese on Banana Nut Bread

Spread about 1 tablespoon of cream cheese on each of the Banana Bread slices. Top with peach slices. Eat!

PEACHES & CREAM CHEESE ON
BANANA NUT BREAD

1/4 cup cream cheese, softened
4 slices Banana Bread (page 87)
1 tree-ripened peach, halved, pitted
*   and sliced*

PEARS

The pear harvest arrives in late August as a sweet punctuation mark to the end of the Oregon summer. First comes the Bartlett, followed by the Comice, Bosc, Anjou, Nelis, Forelle, and Seckel varieties. The harvest ends in October, but pears store so well that you can indulge yourself with them all through the winter.

Grilled Cheese with Oregon Pears

*GRILLED CHEESE WITH
    OREGON PEARS*

*8 slices Squaw Bread (page 161) or
    other whole-grain bread.*

*4 (1/4-inch thick) slices Gruyère cheese,
    cut to fit the bread*

*2 large pears, peeled, cored and thinly
    sliced lengthwise*

1/2 pound thinly sliced smoked ham

*4 (1/4-inch thick) slices provolone
    cheese, cut to fit the bread*

1/4 cup butter, room temperature

On each of 4 slices of bread, layer 1 slice Gruyère, several thin slices pear, several thin slices ham, and 1 slice provolone. Top each sandwich with one of the remaining slices of bread.

Pre-warm and lightly butter a griddle over medium heat. Gently place the sandwiches on the griddle and cook until golden brown on the bottom and the lower slice of cheese has begun to melt. Meanwhile, gently butter the top slices of bread, then turn each sandwich over with a spatula and cook on the second side until it is golden and cheese has melted. Yields 4 servings.

CHERRIES

Thanks to our rich volcanic soil and mild climate, this glorious form of edible art makes a grand entrance every summer for an all-too-brief engagement. For three to six weeks beginning in early July, it is the main attraction in every produce section.

The main types of cherries you'll encounter at market are the dark sweet Bing and Lambert. Less common, but no less delicious, are the the Royal Anne, light-colored, large and firm; the Black Republican, dark red to black, with a distinct flavor; and the Stella, similar to the Lambert in its flavor and color.

For an excellent way to celebrate the season, why not whip up the following elegant little tart? It's another creation by Leif Eric Benson, Timberline Lodge Executive Chef. He probably wouldn't agree, but I think of it as the ultimate open-face sandwich.

Timberline Lodge Sweet Cherry Tart

Combine the water, almond extract, and gelatin in a small bowl. Set aside. Cream the cream cheese, then add the sour cream, half-and-half, and sugar. Melt the gelatin by placing the bowl in very hot water. Stir until dissolved. Add the melted gelatin to the cream cheese mixture.

AMARETTO CREAM

1 tablespoon water

1 teaspoon almond extract

1-1/2 tablespoons (2-1/4 envelopes)
   unflavored gelatin

4 ounces cream cheese

1/2 cup sour cream

2 tablespoons half-and-half

1/4 cup sugar

TART DOUGH

2-3/4 cups flour

1 teaspoon baking powder

2/3 cup sugar

1/2 cup chilled butter

2 eggs

1/2 teaspoon vanilla extract

8 ounces sliced almonds, toasted

CHERRY TOPPING

2 cups Oregon Pinot Noir
  (or other dry red wine)

1 cup water

1/4 cup sugar

4 tablespoons cornstarch

4 cups fresh, pitted Bing cherries
  (or Lamberts, or other dark red,
  sweet cherry)

Combine the flour, baking powder, sugar and butter in the bowl of a food processor. Process in short bursts until the mixture has a crumbly texture. Alternatively, you can cut the butter into the dry ingredients, using a pastry cutter or two knives. Add the eggs, vanilla, and almonds, and combine until just mixed (if using a food processor, process in bursts until a ball is formed).

Press the dough into a 9-inch tart pan with a removable bottom. Prick the surface of the dough using a fork. Line the pastry with aluminum foil. Sprinkle a layer of raw rice about 1/2 inch thick over the foil to hold the pastry down as it begins to cook. Bake in 350° oven for 10 to 15 minutes, then remove foil and continue baking until light golden-brown. Remove from the oven and pour in the Amaretto cream. Chill.

Combine the water, sugar, and cornstarch. Bring the wine to a boil in a saucepan, and stir in the cornstarch mixture. Cook until thickened. Add the cherries and heat briefly. Pour into the chilled tart and refrigerate until served.

Approximate total preparation time: 5 hours, including chilling time. Yields 12 servings.

Source: *Timberline Lodge Cookbook, Northwest Seasonal Recipes,* by Leif Eric Benson, Graphic Arts Center Publishing Co.

ASPARAGUS

If there is order to the universe, then surely asparagus was put on earth for a higher purpose than mere nutritional sustenance. Would spring really be as mandatory if there was no asparagus to be nurtured? It must be more than chance that those lovely green stalks poke through the winter-ravaged ground when they do—reassuring us that waterslides, concerts in the park and ice cream on a stick can't be far behind.

Not that fields of electric-blue irises and tipsy tulips aren't equally worthy harbingers of spring. But asparagus is a symbol you can sink your teeth into. Particularly when it's from the Pacific Northwest. Sweet, and richly hued in deep greens and luxuriant purples, these tender spears can shoot up a startling 8 to 10 inches in one night when the conditions are just right. At least, that's what the growers say. And it's something you want to be out there in the field listening for, they add, because you can actually hear the stalks rattling against each other as they reach for the stars.

In order to enjoy simple recipes, one must start with perfect asparagus—or "grass" as it's lovingly referred to in the field. Then give it the care it deserves during preparation:

- PEEL, DON'T SNAP. It's traditional to bend the lower portion of each stalk until it snaps into edible and inedible portions. This wastes quite a bit of perfectly good asparagus. Better to take a vegetable peeler or paring knife and gently peel down, starting about 4 inches from the tip. Then you'll have to cut off only about 1/2 inch of stalk.

- BLANCH IT. Peeled stalks won't need special asparagus cookers that hold the vegetable upright, because the stalks will cook evenly from tip to base. Use a pot or frying pan large enough to hold asparagus spears horizontally. Fill the pot three-fourths full of water, adding a teaspoon of salt per quart, if desired, and bring to a boil. Add the asparagus, cover just until the water begins to boil again, and then remove the lid. This stops the chlorophyll destruction that turns beautiful green stalks to olive drab.

Reduce the heat and cook for 4 minutes, then begin testing for doneness. The asparagus is done just when it's easily pierced by a sharp knife.

- COOL IT. If you're not going to serve the asparagus immediately, plunge it into cold water to prevent further cooking. Remove the cooled spears with a slotted spoon to a clean towel on a rack; cover and refrigerate until needed (within 24 hours).

Asparagus Rolls with Sesame Mayonnaise

Early in life I once found myself in a luncheon situation where asparagus rolls were the featured course. Being ruled by the vagaries of a youthful palate, I regarded such effrontery as a clear challenge to my mental health. Happily, those days are long gone, and the challenge now is to make the most of the short asparagus season. Variety through creative preparation is the answer. The sauce used here is simple to prepare, and nicely compliments the fresh asparagus in this simple little roll-up.

ASPARAGUS ROLLS WITH
SESAME MAYONNAISE

1/2 cup mayonnaise
1/4 cup sour cream
1/4 teaspoon sesame oil . . .

In a small bowl, combine mayonnaise, sour cream, sesame oil and soy sauce; set aside while assembling the sandwiches (refrigerate if preparing more than 30 minutes ahead). Using a rolling pin, flatten each slice of bread slightly. Spread each slice with some of the sesame mayonnaise. Trim asparagus stalks to fit across the width of the bread. Place one spear on one end of a bread slice and roll up tightly, jelly-roll fashion. Repeat for remaining bread slices. Wrap each roll in a small square of plastic wrap or aluminum foil; refrigerate for 1 hour.

For final assembly of sandwiches: In a small bowl, combine the sesame seeds and minced chives. Unwrap the chilled asparagus rolls and spread a 1/2-inch wide line of butter down the seam side of each roll. Dip the buttered surface in the sesame seed mixture. Serve immediately or refrigerate and serve within 3 hours. Yields 4 servings.

Splash of soy sauce
  (about 1/8 teaspoon)
16 slices whole wheat bread, crusts
  removed
16 fresh asparagus spears, trimmed,
  peeled and blanched as previously
  described
1 tablespoon sesame seeds, lightly
  toasted
1 tablespoon finely minced chives
Softened butter

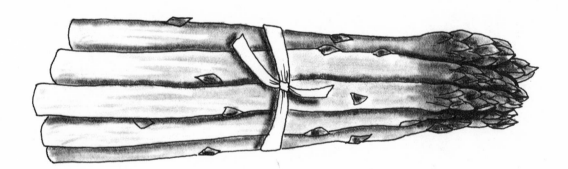

Chapter 2

*O*utdoor Fare

Visualize yourself relaxing in a secluded campground deep within the gentle mountains of western Oregon. Ancient firs standing about with their crowns bathed in waning morning mists give the site a cathedral atmosphere. Kaleidoscopic light-play from moving sun-breaks, imitating the art of stained glass, completes the lovely illusion.

Revel in the peace, and feel the spiritual renewal that nature has to offer. Or, saunter over to the nearby ice-cold stream and have a chuckle at the sight of family and friends wading about on nerve-less legs, dipnets in hand, noses down and fannies up, in search of the wily crawdad. After all, there's more than one brand of spiritual renewal. Sometimes it comes hot and dipped in butter.

Welcome to the great Oregon outdoors. From crawdad expeditions to football tailgate parties, excuses abound to get outside in this state. And since appetites only expand in the fresh air, familiarity with cuisine that will stand up to the absence of walls is not exactly an optional social grace in these parts.

The following set of recipes has something for most any situation, from strenuous hiking to sit-down formality.

Roast Beef & Pepper-Jack Sandwich

There's something special about a picnic. Something even the finest restaurant can't match, short of importing ants, dappled sunlight, twittering birds and a refreshing breeze. Yessir, put me in the great outdoors, simple sandwich in hand, a bottle of wine and my sweetie by my side, and I'm in heaven.

It seems that in the open air, our senses are easily tantalized by less complicated things. So take a cue from nature: Unless you think bears and deer look better in bow-ties, the only garnishes you'll need to round out this sandwich are a little mayonnaise, a few slices of garden-fresh tomatoes, and some pickled Greek pepperoncini.

This sandwich will taste best if you pack all of the ingredients separately and assemble it to suit yourself at the picnic site. Yields 4 servings.

ROAST BEEF & PEPPER-JACK SANDWICH

1 pound thinly-sliced roast beef

1/2 pound thinly-sliced jalapeño pepper-jack cheese

8 thick slices of Squaw Bread (page 161) or other whole grain bread

Garnishes: mayonnaise, tomato slices, pickled Greek pepperoncini

Southwest Shredded Beef Sandwiches

After a 2-hour drive to reach one of our favorite cross-country ski trails, my husband and I weren't about to let freezing temperatures stand in the way of a good time. So we slapped on extra layers of clothing and hoped that we'd soon generate enough body heat to appreciate what a good time we were having.

For the first mile up McKenzie Pass, getting warm meant THINKING warm. I employed every high school drama class technique I knew: I was a toasting marshmallow, a lizard in the Sahara, a beach bum in the Bahamas. By the time we reached the lava flow at Windy Gap, all my fingers and toes had resumed working, but they weren't happy.

We unclamped our skis and scurried out to the bluff for a quick look. Clouds swirled about us, filmy and shredded from the lashing wind. Through the surging mist the alabaster landscape seemed ghostly—a strange emptiness flowing through the forest. After a moment's appreciation, Steve handed me half a candy bar. But the unrelenting chill was already upon us, making my face so cold I couldn't chew. Time to get moving.

Once back at the van we peeled away the frozen layers, stomped our icy boots on the ground and gunned the heater to full blast. But what really restored us the most was the steaming hot spicy beef sandwich filling that we had waiting. Since then, Steve has taken to calling it "Jan's Thermonuclear Sloppy Joes." You be the judge.

SOUTHWEST SHREDDED BEEF SANDWICHES

3 to 3-1/2 pound boneless chuck roast

1 (7 ounce) can diced green chiles

4 tablespoons cumin powder

2 tablespoons chile powder

Salt and pepper

1 cup chopped yellow onion

1 tablespoon salad oil

1 (10 ounce) can diced tomatoes and
  green chiles (I don't usually recom-
  mend brands, but RO-TEL is the one
  you want in this case)

2 (14-1/2 ounce) cans stewed tomatoes

1 cup minced pickled jalapeño slices

1/4 cup chopped fresh cilantro

1 teaspoon salt

12 onion buns

Shredded lettuce

Shredded cheese

Place roast on a sheet of heavy duty aluminum foil (18 inches by 25 inches). Combine the diced green chiles, 2 tablespoons of the cumin powder, chile powder, salt and pepper. Spread the mixture over the top of the roast and then wrap the foil around the roast, sealing well. Place in a baking pan and bake in 325° oven for 3-1/2 to 4 hours, or until the meat is so tender it falls apart. Be careful when unwraping the roast; the steam will burn!

When the meat is done, lift it from the pool of drippings in the foil and allow it to cool on a plate until it is easy to handle. Meanwhile, pour the meat drippings into a small container and skim off the fat. You will have about 1/2 cup of meat juice remaining, which should be reserved.

Shred the cooled roast with a fork or your fingers into small strips and fibers of meat; set aside. A 3-pound roast will yield about 4 cups of shredded meat.

In a large pot, sauté the onion in the salad oil until soft. Add the reserved meat juices, shredded meat, diced tomatoes with green chiles, stewed tomatoes, minced pickled jalapeño peppers, cilantro, remaining 2 table-spoons cumin powder and salt. The mixture will seem very soupy at this point. Simmer gently, uncovered, over medium-high heat until thickened (but still rather saucy), about 30 minutes. Pack immediately into two 1-quart wide-mouth vacuum bottles.

Filling can be prepared ahead of time and then refriger-ated or frozen. When ready to use, thoroughly reheat mixture by bringing it to a boil and simmering about 5 minutes on stove, or microwaving on HIGH until very hot and bubbly, before packing in vacuum bottle.

To assemble sandwiches, partially split each bun length-wise, sprinkle in some of the shredded cheese, then top with a portion of the hot filling, another sprinkling of cheese, and shredded lettuce. Yields 12 servings.

Meatball Sandwiches

In a bowl, combine the bread crumbs and milk and allow to stand until the milk has been soaked up by the crumbs. Add the cheese, egg, onion, parsley, garlic, salt and pepper; mix well. Add the meats and gently mix. Form the meat mixture into 1-inch balls.

Bring the Red Sauce to a hard boil and add the uncooked meatballs. Reduce heat and simmer until the meatballs are cooked, about 45 minutes to 1 hour. During the last 15 minutes, add fresh or dried basil to taste. Immediately pack the meatballs and enough sauce to cover them into a wide-mouth vacuum bottle.

Filling can be prepared ahead of time and refrigerated or frozen until needed. When ready to use, thoroughly reheat mixture by bringing it to a boil and simmering about 5 minutes on stove, or microwaving on HIGH until very hot and bubbly. Pack in a wide-mouth vacuum bottle. Pack the garnishes into a separate container.

To assemble sandwiches, slice the French or Italian rolls part way through lengthwise, and fill each roll with a portion of the meatball mixture. Top with desired garnishes and serve promptly. Yields 4 servings.

MEATBALL SANDWICHES

1 cup fresh bread crumbs

1/4 cup milk

1/3 cup grated Parmesan cheese

1 egg

1/4 cup minced onion

2 tablespoons chopped parsley

1 teaspoon chopped garlic

1/2 teaspoon salt

1/4 teaspoon freshly ground pepper

1/2 pound lean ground beef

1/2 pound ground pork

Red Sauce (recipe follows)

Fresh or dried chopped basil

4 sourdough French or Italian rolls

Sandwich garnishes: slices of cheese (mozzarella, Cheddar or Monterey Jack), pickled pepperoncini, olives, onion rings, lettuce.

RED SAUCE

*1/4 pound finely chopped Italian
    sausage*

1 small onion, chopped

1 cup thinly sliced fresh mushrooms

3 cups tomato sauce

1/2 cup dry red wine

1/3 cup water

1 - 2 teaspoons minced garlic

*1/2 teaspoon each of salt, dried oregano,
    dried basil, and sugar*

In a large pot, brown the sausage. Drain off all but 1 tablespoon of fat, then add onion and mushrooms. Sauté briefly, then add remaining ingredients. Gently simmer uncovered for 20 to 30 minutes. Adjust seasoning to taste. Yields about 3 cups.

Barbecue Dogs with Beer

This may sound like rowdy guests at a tailgate party, but it's considerably more mellow than that.

BARBECUE DOGS WITH BEER

1 cup beer

1 tablespoon Worcestershire sauce

*1/2 cup commercial or homemade
    barbecue sauce*

10 hot dogs, quartered

5 French rolls, split

*Sandwich garnishes: shredded Cheddar
    cheese, chopped yellow or red onion*

In a saucepan, combine beer, Worcestershire sauce, barbecue sauce, and hot dogs. Simmer for 20 minutes. Spoon mixture into a wide-mouth vacuum bottle. To serve, spoon a portion of the filling into each of the rolls. Each diner adds cheese and onion to taste. Yields 5 servings.

Sun-Dried Tomatoes on Swiss

In a bowl, combine sun-dried tomatoes, pickled pepperoncini, olives, Spinach Presto Sauce (or a good pesto) and the 1/4 cup of mayonnaise. Mix well to evenly coat the ingredients with the sauce.

Spread each roll with a little more mayonnaise, then fill with the Swiss cheese and a portion of the sun-dried tomato mixture. Wrap each sandwich with plastic wrap and refrigerate until ready to serve. When packing for picnic, arrange to keep sandwiches well chilled in transit. Yields 4 servings.

SUN-DRIED TOMATOES ON SWISS

1/2 cup chopped sun-dried tomatoes
(well drained)
1/2 cup chopped pickled Greek pepper-
oncini (remove stems before chopping)
1 (2-1/4 ounce) can sliced olives, drained
1/3 cup Spinach Presto Sauce (page 167)
1/4 cup mayonnaise, more as needed
8 slices Swiss cheese
4 French rolls, split

Turkey & Pork Terrine Sandwich

This is a wonderful sandwich for those special picnics or ski trips. It may look complicated, but your food processor makes preparation of the terrine a snap, and it can be done days in advance.

Place the turkey, onion, parsley, eggs, milk, brandy, Worcestershire sauce, garlic, salt and pepper in a food processor and blend for 10 seconds, stopping once to scrape down the sides of the container. Add bread crumbs and continue to purée until mixture is smooth. Transfer this mixture to a bowl and combine with the ground pork, mixing well. To make sure the flavors are balanced, sauté a spoonful of the mixture in a skillet and taste (do not eat the raw mixture); adjust seasonings.

Place the mixture in a 9- by 5-inch loaf pan. Cover the pan with foil, then place in a larger pan partially filled

TURKEY & PORK TERRINE
SANDWICH

1 pound boneless raw turkey breast, cut
into 1-inch chunks
1 medium-sized onion, coarsely chopped
3 tablespoons chopped fresh parsley
2 eggs
2 tablespoons milk
2 tablespoons brandy
1 tablespoon Worcestershire sauce . . .

1 garlic clove, chopped

2 teaspoons salt

1/4 teaspoon freshly ground black pepper

2 cups fresh bread crumbs

1 pound ground pork

2 tomatoes, thinly sliced

Sliced pickles and lettuce for 6 to 8
    sandwiches

Mayonnaise

A good whole-grain German mustard

2 long, slender baguettes

with hot water (the water should reach at least a third of the way up the sides of the inner pan) and bake in a 350° oven for about 1–1/2 hours, or until the juices run clear. Chill the terrine overnight.

To assemble in sandwiches, simply cut baguettes into 5- or 6-inch lengths, then cut each chunk in half lengthwise. Spread halves with mayonnaise and mustard. Layer thin slices of the terrine, pickles, lettuce, and tomatoes on the bottom halves, add the tops, and serve. Yields 6 to 8 servings.

Zesty Veggie French Rolls

ZESTY VEGGIE FRENCH ROLLS

6 French rolls

Olive oil

2 red onions, chopped

2 green onions, chopped

2 cucumbers, peeled and diced

4 large tomatoes, seeded and diced

1 (2-1/4 ounce) can chopped olives

1/3 cup chopped parsley

1/4 cup capers, drained

1 ripe avocado, peeled, seeded and diced

Mayonnaise

Split rolls and carefully scoop out bread from thicker (upper) half of each roll, leaving a shell. Brush insides with olive oil. Combine all remaining ingredients except mayonnaise. Moisten the vegetable mixture with enough mayonnaise to bind it together. Refrigerate until ready to go on hike or picnic, then pack the filling in a chilled wide-mouth vacuum bottle. Just before serving, fill the rolls (if you fill them too soon, they'll get soggy). Yields 6 servings.

On the Trail Delight

This trail bread packs a mighty flavor, making it ideal for quenching a powerful trail hunger. Slice it thin before loading up your pack, then pile with sliced cheeses and meats when you sit down to eat.

Grease a 9- by 5-inch loaf pan. Combine flour, baking powder, onion powder, salt, pepper and soda in a large bowl. Using a fork, mix in the provolone, tomatoes, parsley and basil. In another bowl, whisk together eggs, oil, and garlic. Mix in buttermilk. Add the buttermilk mixture to dry ingredients and stir just until combined. Pour the dough into the prepared pan and sprinkle dehydrated onions over its surface. Bake in a 350° oven until a skewer inserted in center comes out clean, about 50 minutes. Invert onto rack and cool completely. Bread can be prepared up to 3 days ahead if wrapped in foil and refrigerated. Serve at room temperature, thinly sliced. Yields 8 servings.

ON THE TRAIL DELIGHT

2-1/4 cups all purpose flour

2 teaspoons baking powder

2 teaspoons onion powder

1 teaspoon salt

1 teaspoon freshly ground pepper

1/2 teaspoon baking soda

1 cup grated provolone cheese

1/3 cup drained oil-packed sun-dried tomatoes (oil reserved), chopped

1/4 cup chopped fresh parsley

2 teaspoons dried basil, crumbled

2 eggs

5 tablespoons reserved oil from sun-dried tomatoes

2 cloves garlic, peeled and pressed or finely minced

1-1/4 cups buttermilk

1 tablespoon dehydrated onions

Grilled Teriyaki Lamb Strips with Fresh Avocado Relish

Somewhere between "Walkin' in a Winter Wonderland" and "Those Lazy, Crazy, Hazy Days of Summer," Oregon outdoor cooking aficionados awaken. As buds blossom and birds chirp, they scrape months of accumulated cobwebs and grime from their precious Webers. They haul carloads of charcoal home from the store. Then they keep wary eyes on the moody Northwest skies, standing ready to fire up whenever a warming streak of gold punctuates the evening air. While a wonderfully juicy, smokey hamburger is probably foremost in everyone's mind in the beginning, sooner or later alternatives are needed. This is a good one.

GRILLED TERIYAKI LAMB STRIPS
WITH FRESH AVOCADO RELISH

1-1/2 pounds boneless lamb, cut into
  long, 1-inch wide strips
2 medium-sized onions, cut in approxi-
  mately 1-inch wedges or chunks
1/2 cup light soy sauce
1/4 cup brown sugar
1 tablespoon cooking oil
2 teaspoons sesame oil
2 large cloves garlic, minced
1/2 teaspoon ground ginger
4 French rolls, split and toasted over coals
Mayonnaise
Avocado Relish (recipe follows)
Shredded lettuce

Place lamb strips and onion chunks in a large resealable plastic bag, or in a shallow glass pan. Combine the soy sauce, brown sugar, cooking oil, sesame oil, garlic and ginger and pour over the meat and onions. Refrigerate mixture for at least 6 hours, or overnight. To assemble, remove lamb strips from marinade and thread onto bamboo skewers, accordion-fashion, alternating with the onion chunks. Grill over hot coals, turning several times, for about 12 minutes or until meat reaches desired degree of doneness. Brush occasionally with marinade while cooking.

To assemble sandwiches, spread each roll with some mayonnaise, if desired, then add some of the lamb strips and onion chunks. Top with avocado relish and shredded lettuce. Yields 4 servings.

Avocado Relish

Combine all ingredients in a bowl. Cover and refrigerate until ready to use.

AVOCADO RELISH

1 peeled and diced avocado

1 peeled and finely chopped tomato

1/4 cup finely chopped green onion

1/2 green sweet bell pepper, finely chopped

1/2 cup peeled and finely chopped cucumber

2 tablespoons diced green chiles

3 tablespoons fresh lemon juice

1/2 teaspoon salt

1/2 teaspoon Worcestershire sauce

1/8 teaspoon ground pepper

Barbecue Chicken Sandwich

Place whole chicken in a large kettle, cover with water and heat to boiling. Simmer until chicken is cooked, about 45 minutes to 1 hour. Remove from pot, cool until easy to handle, and then remove meat from bones. You will have about 3 cups of shredded chicken.

Meanwhile, sauté onion in the butter until soft and transparent. Add water, vinegar, Worcestershire, lemon juice, brown sugar, chile sauce, salt and paprika. Simmer for 10 minutes. Add shredded chicken and simmer an additional 10 minutes. Pack immediately into a 1-quart wide-mouth vacuum bottle.

Filling can be prepared ahead and then refrigerated or frozen until needed. When ready to use, thoroughly reheat mixture by bringing it to a boil and simmering

BARBECUE CHICKEN SANDWICH

1 whole 3 to 3-1/2 pound fryer

1/3 cup chopped onions

1 tablespoon butter or margarine

2/3 cup water

3 tablespoons vinegar

2 tablespoons Worcestershire sauce

1/3 cup lemon juice

3 tablespoons brown sugar

1 (12-ounce) jar chile sauce

1 teaspoon salt

1/4 teaspoon paprika

6 onion or sesame hamburger buns

about 5 minutes on stove, or microwaving on HIGH until very hot and bubbly, before packing in vacuum bottle.

To assemble sandwiches, split open each bun and fill with a portion of the hot filling. Yields 6 servings.

Johnny Burgers

This is so simple to throw together that most people don't even think about it. But it's great for situations where time may be limited, such as at tailgate parties.

JOHNNY BURGERS

*6 boned and skinned chicken breast
   halves*

Salt

Lemon pepper

6 French rolls, split

Mayonnaise

*Lettuce, tomato slices and onions
   for garnish*

Grill chicken breasts over hot coals, turning several times, until cooked through and golden, about 10 minutes. Season with salt and lemon pepper. If desired, toast the rolls over coals too. Prepare each roll with mayonnaise and preferred garnishes, then add chicken breast. Yields 6 servings.

TERIYAKI ALTERNATIVE

Marinate chicken breasts in Teriyaki Sauce (page 173, or your own concoction) for 30 minutes before grilling.

MENUS

A SIMPLE TAILGATE AFFAIR

Fresh-fried Tortilla Chips with Guacamole (page 169)
Summer Gazpacho Soup (page 159)

Johnny Burgers (page 42)
Tossed Green Salad of Mixed Greens, Sunflower Seeds
And Tarragon Vinaigrette (page 172)

Chocolate Cake

SUPPER BY A STREAM

Frozen Strawberry Daiquiris (page 174)
Roasted Hazelnuts and Garlic Butter Croutons (page 162)

Roast Beef & Pepper-Jack Sandwich (page 32)
Fresh Vegetables with Pocket Delight Vinaigrette Dip (page 169)

Fresh Fruit and Sugar Cookies

Chapter 3

*O*regon Heroes

*H*ave you ever wondered where the term "hero sandwich" comes from? No? Well, I hadn't either until I decided to include some hero sandwiches in this book. My best guess is that the term refers to the scale of such creations, which tend to rival the fictional heroes of mankind for extravagance. Of course, this definition will never do in a book of sober reflections on the glories of Oregon on a bun. So I have decided on a reasonable alternative. The Hero Sandwich is an officially sanctioned (by me) vehicle for recognizing a small sample of the many admirable Oregonians who have contributed greatly to the spirit, image, or well-being of their state and its people. It is the only award I know of that is equally adaptable to artists, athletes, politicians, and picklers.

JEAN AUEL

In her middle years—at a stage when many people are settling in and thinking, "Okay, so maybe I'll never be a brain surgeon (or a ballerina, or marathon runner)"—Jean Auel walked away from her career path and wrote a best-selling novel. Her Cro-Magnon heroine in *The Clan of the Cave Bear,* Ayla, who broke free of her Neanderthal lifestyle to find true fulfillment in the Ice Age, took America and at least 22 other countries by storm.

It was Auel's ability to weave extensive research into a good yarn that brought this prehistoric period to life for millions of readers who had never seen the inside of an anthropology text, let alone a cave. The first three novels in her Earth's Children series have racked up a staggering 233 weeks on the New York Times best seller list. With three more installments to go before Ayla's story has been fully told, Auel's best-seller status looks to be a fairly permanent thing. At least for this century.

Auel once told a reporter that she didn't care whether or not people knew her, as long as they read her books. But with *The Clan of the Cave Bear, The Valley of Horses,* and *The Mammoth Hunters,* you can't help getting an inkling of who she is—or at least a peek at her immutable faith in womankind, and mankind.

The consensus among those who knew that Jean Auel was one of my Oregon Heroes was that the main ingredient in her sandwich should be raw beef. Steak Tartare, maybe? Garnished with a few wild hickory nuts and spring greens? Something a Neanderthal could love.

Tempting. But I decided to take another tack. After all, this is a modern woman who turned the publishing world upside down. She and her husband have been able to build a dream of a house on the northern Oregon coast, so the sandwich I've created for Auel is one befitting that lifestyle. It's elegant, yet laced with the earthy essence of Oregon's coastal fare.

Crab Cakes with North Coast Tartar Sauce

Combine the egg, whipping cream, soda crackers, mustard, pepper, pepper sauce, parsley and chives. Toss the crabmeat with the flour, then combine with the egg mixture. Form into 6 round patties.

Heat butter in a large heavy skillet over medium-high heat until bubbly. Add crab cakes, in batches if necessary to avoid overcrowding, and cook until golden brown, about 3 minutes on each side. Drain on paper towels and keep hot in oven until all 6 cakes are cooked.

To assemble sandwiches, spread both sides of each bun with some of the North Coast Tartar Sauce. Place a crab-cake on the bottom half, then top with the lettuce, toma-toes and onion rings (as desired), add top bun and serve. Yields 6 servings.

*CRAB CAKES WITH NORTH COAST
  TARTAR SAUCE*

1 egg
1/4 cup whipping cream
1/4 cup crushed soda crackers
1 teaspoon dry mustard
1/4 teaspoon white pepper
Several dashes hot pepper sauce
1 tablespoon minced fresh parsley
1 tablespoon snipped chives
*1 pound freshly-cooked Dungeness
  crabmeat, flaked*
3 tablespoons flour
1/4 cup butter
6 onion sandwich buns, toasted
*North Coast Tartar Sauce
  (recipe follows)*
*Shredded lettuce, sliced tomatoes and
  onion rings for garnish*

NORTH COAST TARTAR SAUCE

1/2 cup sour cream

1/2 cup mayonnaise

1 hard-cooked egg, peeled and minced

1/4 cup each: finely minced celery,
  dill pickle

2 tablespoons finely minced onion

2 to 3 teaspoons fresh lemon juice

1/2 teaspoon grated lemon peel

1/4 teaspoon dried dillweed

Salt and freshly ground pepper to taste

In a small bowl, combine ingredients; adjust seasonings and chill until ready to serve. Yields about 1-1/2 cups sauce.

WILL VINTON

Anyone who injects charm and wit into prime time television advertising is a hero to me. Enter Will Vinton and team, who have discovered within little blobs of clay such media giants as the California Raisins and that nemesis of hot pizza, The Noid.

Claymation® is the term Vinton uses to describe his art of clay animation. Now it's a registered trademark and a whoppingly successful industry. Based in Portland, Oregon, Vinton's 43,000 square-foot studio complex attracts talented young artists like north attracts a compass needle. They are drawn to become a part of the dream, the vision. You see, within the film and advertising communities Vinton has another name: "The Disney of the Pacific Northwest." The comparison is inevitable, considering the plethora of commercial and historical characters—from animated athletic shoes and dancing cereal boxes to Mark Twain, that he has trotted out over the years.

His less commercial ventures have also been successful. *Closed Mondays* won the 1975 Academy Award for Best Animated Short Film. That was when Will Vinton Productions got rolling. In the years that followed, there were more Oscar nominations for his short films *Rip Van Winkle, The Creation,* and *The Great Cognito,* as well as one for Best Visual Effects for the Disney feature, *Return to Oz.*

The Raisins have taken on lives of their own, generating about $500 million in merchandise, starring in their own television shows, and jetting off to Europe for a "Meet the Raisins" special.

With all that he has accomplished, Vinton continues to look ahead and to hold the creative edge that sets his work apart. Even his worry lines—the unavoidable badge of success worn by pioneers of industry—have their own unique shape. It's called a smile.

The Will Vinton Pizza Sandwich

Pizza??? One might think something incorporating RAISIN bread more appropriate. But Will says that even though the California Raisins have been very good to him, his favorite character is The Noid, that rubber-faced, pizza-stomping fiend. So here's a pizza sandwich even The Noid could love.

THE WILL VINTON PIZZA SANDWICH

1 loaf French bread, measuring approximately 15 inches long, 4 inches wide, and 3 inches high

3/4 pound Italian sausage, crumbled and browned

3 tablespoons sliced olives (half of a 2-1/4 ounce can)

1/4 pound thinly sliced mozzarella cheese

1/2 cup spaghetti sauce (any commercially canned variety will do)

2 ounces thinly sliced pepperoni

1/2 yellow onion, thinly sliced

About 5 fresh mushrooms, thinly sliced

1 small green sweet bell pepper, thinly sliced

Parmesan cheese

1 cup shredded medium or sharp Cheddar cheese

Sandwich garnishes: thinly sliced tomatoes, shredded lettuce, vinaigrette dressing

With a serrated knife, cut the loaf of bread in half lengthwise, creating a slightly thicker bottom half. With your fingers, gently hollow out the bottom half, leaving a 1/2-inch border around the edge, and about 1/2-inch thickness on the bottom.

Place both halves face up on a baking sheet and broil until golden. Remove from oven and spread half of the mozzarella slices along the bottom of the hollowed out portion. Next, layer on the sausage and olives, then drizzle on the spaghetti sauce. On top of the sauce, layer the pepperoni, remaining mozzarella, onions, mushrooms, and pepper rings.

At this point, the sandwich can be wrapped in plastic and refrigerated up to 2 hours. About 15 minutes before serving, place the lower portion of the sandwich on a baking sheet. Sprinkle it with Parmesan cheese and then bake in a 400° oven for 5 to 8 minutes, until very hot and slightly golden around the edges. Meanwhile, sprinkle the toasted face of the top half of loaf with the shredded Cheddar. Place in oven alongside the lower portion and continue baking another 5 minutes.

Remove both halves from the oven. Arrange a few sliced tomatoes and some shredded lettuce atop each one. Drizzle the lettuce with a little of your favorite vinaigrette (or just a little oil and vinegar), then put the two halves together. Cut the loaf into 4 pieces, secure them with bamboo skewers if necessary, and serve immediately. Yields 4 servings.

JAMES BEARD

James Beard, the preeminent master of American cuisine, never forgot his Oregon roots. Although an entire nation of Beard worshippers—from Manhattan to San Francisco—felt he belonged to them, Beard returned often to his home town of Gearhart on the Oregon coast to replenish his soul and revel in the Pacific Northwest bounty. While in Oregon, he taught, and explored, and sought out promising young chefs and exciting new restaurants.

Of course, he did belong to the country, in the sense that he provided direction at a time when American cuisine had no coherence. Perhaps it began in 1946 when he pioneered the first television cooking school. Viewers seemed to understand that his impeccable taste was based in a sincere appreciation of quality, rather than snobbery.

When Beard himself reflected on his love of food in one of his many books, *Delights and Prejudices,* he recalled how tastes he experienced in his youth marked him for life. While his extraordinary young palate explored essences of succulent Dungeness crab, wild berries, and prized razor clams, he was unknowingly absorbing impressions that would ultimately be shared with the world.

Through the efforts of The James Beard Foundation, Beard's house in Greenwich Village has been maintained as a national gathering place for his followers and colleagues. It has become a research center for American food and wine; an official meeting place for non-profit culinary organizations. Classes are once again offered in his famous kitchen, scholarships are awarded, and a number of support programs are ongoing. In this manner, Beard's role as generous mentor of new talent lives on. If you would like to become a supporter of the Foundation, membership information can be obtained by writing to The James Beard Foundation, 167 West 12th Street, New York, New York 10011.

There are many ingredients that could logically be used in a James Beard sandwich, because Beard was not one to concern himself with fads and fashion. He was as comfortable around a bowl of steamed clams fresh from Tillamook Bay as he was with an exquisite pâté fois gras. Food just had to be good—both in the quality of the raw ingredients and execution of the recipe.

Take the hamburger, for instance. It could be a delicious morsel, he said, if the beef was good, contained an appropriate amount of fat, and was cooked properly so that it retained its juices. Beard observed that most hamburgers were grilled over excessively high heat, leaving the meat charred and tough on the outside, and dry and flavorless on the inside.

He loved the way his mother would prepare them, seasoned with generous amounts of fresh garlic; and also found it a treat to mix in coarsely grated Cheddar cheese, shallots, Worcestershire, mustard and Maggi Seasoning. Then he'd grill it in butter and serve it on a good bun with a tasty relish.

So a Beard Burger it is. If you make it, you must use only the finest beef available; well-aged, so when you grill it gently over medium-hot coals, or sauté it in butter, the flavor of the excellent meat comes through. You'll also use a good-quality Oregon Cheddar in your burger, and top it with a nice thick slab of another Pacific Northwest specialty, the Walla Walla Sweet onion. My only wish is that Mr. Beard was still around so I could serve it up in person.

The James Beard Burger

Combine the ground sirloin with the shallots, Worcestershire, mustard, salt and pepper. Gently shape the mixture into 4 patties. Melt about 1 tablespoon of butter in a skillet over medium-high heat. Add patties and sauté slowly, until cooked to desired doneness, turning once after first side is browned. When patties are almost done, top them with cheese slices so cheese will have time to melt slightly.

Serve hamburgers on buns dressed with condiments by diners. Yields 4 servings.

THE JAMES BEARD BURGER

1-1/2 pounds sirloin, ground (pick out a
  nicely marbled slab of sirloin in the
  meat case and have your butcher grind
  it for you; it will be tender and juicy)
1/2 cup finely minced shallots
1 tablespoon Worcestershire sauce
2 teaspoons Dijon mustard
1 teaspoon salt
Freshly ground black pepper
Butter
4 thick slices medium or sharp Cheddar
  cheese
4 bakery-fresh hamburger buns, toasted
4 thick slices Walla Walla Sweet onion
  (or other sweet Spanish-style onion)
Additional condiments: mustard, mayonnaise, homemade relish, ketchup,
  tomatoes, lettuce

JAMES DePREIST

It's hard to overestimate the value of a person like James DePreist to a state coming of age in the arts. This is a time for setting high expectations, and fostering a tradition of fulfilling them, as artistic resources and public support grow through barriers to quality. In a place to which so many people are bound by appreciation for beauty, the sky should be the limit.

Since being named Music Director of the Oregon Symphony in 1980, DePreist has captivated Oregonians with his talent, charisma, and energy. Even those with a limited knowledge of "the arts" suddenly were aware of the Symphony and its dynamic leader.

In the last decade, DePreist has transformed an orchestra of regional interest into one of national significance. His first recordings with the Oregon Symphony have met with critical acclaim. In arranging and conducting the musical soundtrack for "The Cosby Show's" 1988 season, he stretched the orchestra's horizon beyond the traditional, and brought its sound to an audience of 62 million.

DePreist is also an inveterate guest conductor, being much in demand by major orchestras throughout the United States and Europe, where he reflects much credit on his home. In his spare time, he has written two books of poetry.

So what kind of sandwich should bear the name of James DePreist? Since he was born in Philadelphia, my first inclination was to create something along the lines of a Philly sandwich—a rich concoction of sautéed onions and beef. But that alone seemed a little too pedestrian. And so, for color, flair and zest, I added sun-dried tomatoes, crisp bell pepper rings, fresh basil, and just a few pickled peppers.

I think you'll find it as direct and tantalizing as the man and his music.

The De Preist Delight

In a small pan, sauté onion in the olive oil over medium heat until soft and translucent; remove from heat. Spread the French roll halves with mayonnaise and mustard to taste. Layer with the roast beef, sautéed onions, pepper rings, sun-dried tomatoes, basil and pepperoncini. Add a few leaves of romaine lettuce for garnish, if desired. Yields 1 sandwich.

THE DePREIST DELIGHT

1/2 yellow onion, thinly sliced

1 to 2 tablespoons olive oil (preferably oil drained from the sun-dried tomatoes)

1 French roll, split and toasted

Mayonnaise

Coarse-grained German-style mustard

4 ounces of deli-style sliced roast beef

4 or 5 thinly sliced red and green sweet bell pepper rings

4 or 5 sun-dried tomatoes, well-drained

2 or 3 sprigs fresh basil, chopped

3 pickled Greek pepperoncini (pierce each pepper and drain, if necessary)

Romaine lettuce leaves for garnish

DOC SEVERINSEN

Doc Severinsen has come a long way from his boyhood days in the rural town of Arlington, Oregon, where he was nicknamed "Little Doc" after his father, Dr. Carl Severinsen. But that is where the flamboyant musical director of "The Tonight Show" first exhibited his artistic tendencies. At the age of seven, Severinsen announced his plans to take up the trombone. However, when he went to the local music store to make his purchase, the only horn available was a trumpet. Three weeks later, after studying a lesson book and being tutored by his father—a gifted amateur violinist in his own right—Little Doc was invited to join the high school band. By the age of twelve, he won the first of many awards, the Music Educator's National Contest. While still in high school he hit the road with the Ted Fio Rito Orchestra.

Severinsen's horn was his passion. Once it also became his profession, he toured with the Tommy Dorsey, Benny Goodman and Charlie Barnet bands. In 1949 he became an NBC staff musician, joining the Tonight Show Orchestra in 1962. By 1967 he was its musical director.

One can only speculate about how his life would have turned out if there had been a trombone for sale in that little Arlington store. But with the trumpet Severinsen has made more than 25 recordings, and been voted Top Brass Player ten times in Playboy's prestigious music poll. In 1987 he received a Grammy for Best Jazz Instrumental Performance (Big Band).

Obviously, any sandwich creation for Doc Severinsen has to be as colorful and dynamic as his music and his dress. Doc especially likes to cook Italian, so I thought something with a pizza base would be appropriate. But instead of a traditional pizza dough, I simplified the recipe by using focaccia bread, which has become readily available in supermarkets over the last couple of years.

My goal was to meld his Oregon roots with California cuisine—a fresh and inventive style of cooking that parallels Doc's fresh and somewhat free-spirited approach to performance. So I studied that king of L.A. cuisine, Wolfgang Puck, the chef who re-invented pizza through his use of fresh, unconventional ingredients. Things like goat cheese, caviar, and salmon.

Well, no self-respecting Oregon boy would tolerate caviar on his pizza. But the Doc Severinsen Pizza is, shall we say, flamboyant.

The Doc Severinsen Pizza

Place the focaccia bread in a spring-form pan (with removable sides). The loaf should fit snugly so the toppings will stay on its surface when baked.

In a large skillet, sauté the bell peppers and garlic in 1/4 cup of the olive oil until the peppers are softened. Stir in the tomatoes, duxelles, sherry, pepper, and salt; continue cooking until the mixture is thickened, about 7 or 8 minutes. The sauce should be highly seasoned, but not too salty, since the prosciutto is very salty.

Meanwhile, in a small cup, combine the red pepper flakes and oregano with the remaining 1/4 cup of olive oil; brush the mixture over the surface of the focaccia bread. Combine the cheeses in a separate bowl, mixing well.

Spoon about half of the tomato mixture over the surface of the bread, then layer with about three-fourths of the mixed cheeses. Add remaining tomato mixture, then

THE DOC SEVERINSEN PIZZA

1 (8- or 9-inch) round of focaccia bread (available in brown 'n serve form in most supermarkets)

1 green and 1 yellow sweet bell pepper, sliced into thin rings

2 to 3 cloves garlic, peeled and minced

1/2 cup olive oil

8 medium-sized Roma tomatoes, peeled, cored and coarsely chopped

1/2 cup duxelles (page 168)

1/3 cup dry sherry

1/2 teaspoon white pepper

1/4 teaspoon salt

1 tablespoon dried red pepper flakes . . .

1/2 teaspoon dried oregano, crumbled

1/4 pound mozzarella cheese, grated
(2 cups)

1/4 pound fontina cheese, grated (2 cups)

2 ounces provolone cheese, grated (1 cup)

3 ounces alder-smoked Columbia River
salmon, flaked (optional)

3 ounces prosciutto, julienned

1/2 Walla Walla sweet onion, cut into
thin rings

About 1/2 cup finely chopped fresh basil

Parmesan cheese

top with the salmon flakes, prosciutto, onion, and basil. Sprinkle with remaining 3-cheese mixture, sprinkle generously with Parmesan cheese, and bake in 375° oven for about 40 minutes. The top will be golden and bubbly and the bread thoroughly cooked. Remove from oven and allow to sit for at least 20 minutes in the spring-form pan so the juices will settle and the topping will stay together when the ring is finally removed.

Serve warm, at room temperature, or chilled. Yields 6 or 7 generous servings.

The Doc Severinsen Delight makes a marvelous light supper, with a hearty tossed salad of romaine lettuce, Greek olives, freshly grated Parmesan and good-quality vinaigrette. Or...as fantastic picnic fare at your next outdoor jazz festival.

TERRY BAKER

A sculpted chunk of sports history sits in a glass case on the Oregon State University campus. It's a Heisman Trophy, the most prestigious award in college football. And Terry Baker was the man responsible for putting it there in 1962. Also in that trophy case is a copy of the January 7, 1963 issue of *Sports Illustrated*. It's the "Sportsman of the Year" issue, with Baker's portrait on the cover.

It was a remarkable year. A year when good things happened to a fine young honor student in mechanical engineering who also happened to be without peer in the collegiate football ranks. The Beavers ended the season with a 9-2 record, including a victory over Villanova in the Liberty Bowl in which the only points resulted from a 99-yard touchdown run by—you guessed it—Terry Baker.

When it was all over, Baker had garnered practically every football award available to a quarterback. He was named to 12 All-American first teams, and given 21 individual awards, including the Maxwell Award for Outstanding Player in the Nation, the Associated Press and United Press International Player of the Year awards, the Helms Foundation's Top Athlete in North America award, and the Football Foundation Hall of Fame's Scholar-Athlete award. Prior to being selected first in the ensuing NFL draft, Baker kept in shape by captaining the OSU basketball team through a season culminating in a Final Four berth at the NCAA Tournament.

When Baker finally left competitive athletics after several years in professional football, he didn't leave his winning attitude in the locker room. He had already earned a law degree from USC during the off-seasons of his career with the Los Angeles Rams. Admitted to the Oregon State Bar in 1968, he is now a respected Portland attorney. In 1970, he took a leave of absence to work on the staff of President Nixon's Commission on Campus Unrest, and on the Kent State Task Force. Through the early 80's he participated on the Governor's Council for Health, Fitness and Sports, and served on the Salvation Army Harbor Light Center's Advisory council. He serves on a number of boards in the region, including the Lake Oswego School Board, the Lewis & Clark chapter of the March of Dimes, and OSU's Alumni Board.

Back in 1962, the pass combination of Terry Baker to Vern Burke was considered magic. What they did with a pigskin made grown men cry. Baker led the nation in passing and total offense; Burke broke the NCAA record for receptions and yards gained. What better sandwich for this Oregon Hero than...

The Baker-Burke Combo

A winning combination of flavors makes this sandwich a football tailgater's delight. On the side, some folks might enjoy a zesty "Liberty Bowl" of Chili.

THE BAKER-BURKE COMBO

1-1/2 to 2 pounds pork tenderloin
1/2 cup commercial tempura sauce
1/2 cup water
1/2 cup butter
2 tablespoons prepared Chinese hot mustard
1 teaspoon Worcestershire sauce
6 French rolls, split and toasted
Tenderloin Sauce (recipe follows)
Sandwich garnishes: shredded sharp Cheddar cheese, Walla Walla Sweet onion rings (or red Bermuda onions), tomato slices (when in season)

Place the tenderloin in a shallow, narrow container (or resealable plastic bag). In another bowl, combine the tempura sauce and water. Pour all but 2 tablespoons of the marinade over the tenderloin and marinate in refrigerator at least 3 hours, at most overnight. Remove the tenderloin from the marinade. In a small pan, combine the butter, mustard, Worcestershire sauce, and 1/3 cup of the tempura marinade. Heat gently to melt the butter; remove from heat.

To grill, brush the tenderloin with some of the tempura butter, then place it over hot coals. After 5 minutes, brush with the tempura butter, then turn so the top side is now on the bottom, and baste again. After 5 more minutes, baste, then turn the tenderloin onto one of the uncooked sides; baste again. After about 3 minutes, baste, then turn the tenderloin onto its remaining uncooked side; baste and cook about 3 more minutes. Total cooking time will be about 16 minutes at this point, which should be sufficient. If not, cook about 2 more minutes. Remove from grill, and let stand for 5 minutes (meat will continue cooking until it cools somewhat, so don't overcook it on the coals).

To serve, cut the tenderloin crosswise into 1/2-inch

thick slices. Prepare each bun by spreading with some of the Tenderloin Sauce. Place slices of the meat in each prepared bun, then have guests add garnishes and extra sauce as desired. Yields 6 servings.

Combine ingredients in a small bowl. Refrigerate until ready to serve. Yields 1-1/8 cup.

TENDERLOIN SAUCE

1/2 cup sour cream
1/2 cup mayonnaise
2 tablespoons reserved tempura
    marinade

U.S. SENATOR MARK HATFIELD

The Oregon State Capital was familiar territory for Senator Hatfield long before it played such an integral role in his political career. He graduated from Salem High School in 1940, then went on to earn his Bachelor of Arts at Willamette University, a short walk from the Capitol Building. In fact, the only portion of his formal education to take place outside of Salem was during the years he earned his Master of Arts degree at Stanford University in Palo Alto, California.

So it's not surprising that the Oregon State Capital became his workplace for many years as well. First, as a State Representative in 1951, then as a State Senator, Secretary of State, and finally, from 1959 to 1966, as Governor. During these 15 years he was instrumental in the development of Oregon's magnificent system of state parks, in expanding the state's community college system, in creating the Oregon Graduate Center for biological and technological research, and in diversifying Oregon's economy.

In 1966, Hatfield was elected to the United States Senate. By 1980 he had risen to chairmanship of the Senate Appropriations Committee, from which position he worked tirelessly for six years for fiscal responsibility and against centralization of excessive power in the hands of government or business institutions. His many committee assignments and other involvements continue to bring his influence to bear on numerous issues of social services, natural resources management, energy regulation and conservation, labor, and commerce. But he is perhaps best known as a courageous and tireless proponent of peace, disarmament, and humanitarianism throughout the world.

In the Senate, Hatfield has continued to make things happen for Oregon. Through his efforts, Oregon boasts the Marine Science Center at Newport, as well as the Institute for Advanced Biomedical Research at the Oregon Health Sciences University in Portland. Hatfield's concern for an efficient transportation system has helped lead to the Portland light rail project, a superb state highway system, healthy coastal ports, and the Columbia-Snake waterway for moving much of the Northwest's immense harvest. He has worked hard to improve management of Oregon's crucial forestry industry, while preserving the state's unparalleled natural beauty.

Enlightened management of the quality of Oregon's freshwater resources, and the fostering of marine and freshwater fisheries research programs—these abiding interests of Mark Hatfield combine to nurture what I consider to be the shimmering soul of Nature's gifts to this state—the revered salmon. And so, salmon it is...

Salmon & Eggs Benedict

Sauté the mushrooms, shallots and fennel in the butter until mushrooms have released their liquid and the mixture is reduced. Add the sherry, capers, hot pepper sauce, pepper, and salt, and continue cooking until liquid is reduced again and mixture is thickened. Adjust · seasonings, then push the vegetables to one side of the pan. Add the salmon fillets (you may need to add a little more butter to keep them from sticking), and continue cooking, turning them once after about 2 minutes, until fillets are cooked through, about 5 minutes total time. Fish can be easily flaked with a fork when done.

To assemble, place one fillet on each of the toasted English muffin halves. Divide the vegetable mixture between the two servings, then top each with a poached egg and a dollop of Hollandaise Sauce. Add fresh dill weed sprigs for garnish and serve. Yields 2 servings.

SALMON & EGGS BENEDICT

1 cup thinly sliced mushrooms
1/2 cup minced shallots
1/4 cup minced fennel bulb
3 tablespoons butter
1/4 cup dry sherry
2 teaspoons capers
1/4 teaspoon hot pepper sauce
1/4 teaspoon white pepper
1/4 teaspoon salt, more to taste
1 English muffin, split, toasted and
*   buttered*
2 (3 or 4 ounces each) salmon fillets
2 poached eggs
2 generous dollops of Hollandaise Sauce
*   (page 9)*
Garnish with fresh dill weed sprigs

ANGUS BOWMER

On a warm August night, in the little Southern Oregon town of Ashland, a 10-year-old girl sat transfixed as *A Midsummer Night's Dream* gently and oh-so-magically unfolded before her eyes. The stars above the open-air theater glittered as the players cast their golden spell.

It's a night I've never forgotten, even though it took place a long time ago. But for my brother and me it's like yesterday. The only way our parents were able to get us to The Oregon Shakespearean Festival that year

("SHAKE-spear? Yuck!") was with a bribe. After the plays, they promised, we'd spend the rest of our vacation at Diamond Lake. But once Titania, Queen of the Fairies, and the mischievous Puck had captured our hearts, Mom and Dad knew that fishing trips would no longer be a necessary lure. Since then, we have enticed our own children to Ashland, and watched as they too were enthralled by the Bard.

To be sure, this story is not unique. For Angus Bowmer, founder of the Oregon Shakespearean Festival, hooking audiences was a specialty. Beginning the summer of 1935, as a two-play, three-day event on a makeshift Elizabethan platform, he somehow knew that his little theater was a dream worth pursuing. Worth dedicating one's life to build.

And build he did. Even though the original stage was destroyed by fire in 1940, and World War II forced a six-year hiatus, the Oregon Shakespearean Festival resumed production in 1947, this time with an elaborate stagehouse, complete with scene and costume shops. More productions were added to the summer schedule and the company grew.

In 1958 there was another step back when the theater was declared a fire hazard by the Ashland fire marshal. It was razed, and the current Elizabethan Stage, designed by the Festival's resident designer, Richard L. Hay, was built in its place. Banners flown along Main street now invited visitors to "Stay Four Days—See Four Plays"—and everyone did.

More growth was required to meet the demand. So, in 1970, The Angus Bowmer Theater opened with a production of *Rosencrantz and Guildenstern are Dead,* by British playwright Tom Stoppard. This modern indoor theater provided a new direction for the Festival, expanding its season into the spring and fall months when outdoor theater was impossible. In 1977, an intimate third theater, the Black Swan, was added. Directors and actors were now able to give flight to experimental productions of worthy plays not practical for the larger stages, but which leave Black Swan audiences groping for superlatives.

Angus Bowmer, a motivating force to the very end, died in May of 1979. In the 8-month season that followed, his Festival produced 11 plays for 574 performances before 264,054 people. In 1983 it received a Tony Award for Outstanding Regional Theater. Two years later, it celebrated its 50th anniversary, and welcomed its five millionth visitor. Then in 1987, in the Bowmer spirit of taking on new challenges, the Festival's Board of Directors accepted an invitation from the Portland Center for the Performing Arts to establish a resident theater in Portland. As the curtain rose on November 12, 1988 on George Bernard Shaw's *Heartbreak House*, the Oregon Shakespearean Festival became the largest not-for-profit theater in the country.

Jerry Turner, the Festival's Producing Director, once observed that, "The great secret Angus Bowmer had, and which he shared with his public, was that a theater deals with human commonplaces accessible to us all. Somehow, in the works of Shakespeare and in all the great plays of all the great playwrights, there are human truths that need expression so we all can know, most vividly, what it is to be alive."

Of course, for one 10-year-old little girl, all it took was a warm summer night when the air was filled with fairy dust.

Ashland is a picnic-lover's haven, from beautiful Lithia Park adjacent to the Elizabethan Theater, to nearby streams, lakes and hillsides. Perfect pre-theater picnic fare would be this Chinese spring roll, with its succulent ham and vegetable filling all wrapped up and ready to go.

Lithia Park Spring Rolls

LITHIA PARK SPRING ROLLS

2 tablespoons oil

1 cup chopped onion

1/2 cup chopped leek

1 cup thinly sliced celery

1 jalapeño chile, seeded and minced

2 cloves garlic, minced or pressed

1/2 teaspoon minced fresh ginger

1 pound smoked ham, julienne cut

2 cups finely shredded cabbage

1 (5-ounce) can bamboo shoots,
  julienne cut

3 tablespoons sherry

1 tablespoon soy sauce

1 tablespoon cornstarch

1 (1 pound) package egg roll skins

1 egg, beaten

Oil

Heat the 2 tablespoons of oil in a large frying pan or wok. Add the onion, leek, celery, chile, garlic and ginger. Stir-fry for about 1 minute, then add the ham, cabbage and bamboo shoots, and continue to stir-fry for an additional 3 or 4 minutes. Blend together the sherry, soy sauce and cornstarch. Stir the mixture into the vegetables and cook just until thickened. Do not overcook the ingredients or the vegetables will not be crunchy. Remove from heat, adjust seasonings and cool thoroughly before proceeding with recipe.

For each spring roll, place an egg roll skin on counter, with a corner pointing toward you. Arrange about 2 rounded tablespoons of the filling diagonally across the skin, to within 1 inch of the left and right corners. Fold the corner nearest you over the filling. Brush a dot of beaten egg on the left and right corners, then fold these corners in over the filling, pressing them firmly down onto the previously folded corner. Now roll the package to within 1 inch of the top corner. Dot top corner with egg and press it down on the roll to seal. As each spring roll is completed, cover it with plastic wrap until ready to fry. Rolls can be refrigerated up to 12 hours before frying.

Fry a few spring rolls at a time in about 2 inches of hot oil until golden, turning to evenly brown on all sides.

After frying, drain well on paper towels and serve immediately, or refrigerate for later use. Spring rolls are equally delicious hot or cold.

Cooked spring rolls can also be covered and frozen. To reheat frozen rolls, place them on a baking sheet and bake in a 375° oven for about 20 minutes, or microwave on HIGH until heated through.

SENATOR BOB PACKWOOD

Politically speaking, Oregon is a tough nut to crack. Republicans don't follow as straight a conservative line as their national counterparts, and so-called liberals tend to lean a little bit to the right on a lot of issues. Anyone who can get elected to the United States Senate term after term under such conditions must be doing something right.

Senator Packwood is. For one thing, he's a classic Oregonian, which makes him somewhat of a loner. He goes his own way and does what he thinks is right. He's an independent thinker—just like Oregonians in general—and crusades for what he believes in. Women's rights, for example.

In essence, Bob Packwood mirrors his constituents, even down to his love for the outdoors and sense of duty to protect the environment. Such traits placed him on the political path early in his career. His first experience was in 1957, as law clerk to Chief Justice Harold J. Warner of the Oregon Supreme Court. He then practiced law in Portland for ten years, and served three terms in the Oregon legislature. In 1968, exhibiting the adventurous spirit of his great grandfather William H. Packwood, a pioneer and member of the Oregon Constitutional Convention of 1857, Packwood struck out from his secure base in the Oregon Legislature to challenge the formidable Wayne Morse for his long-held seat in the U.S. Senate. On winning, Packwood became that organization's youngest member. Twenty-two years later he is the ranking Republican and former Chairman of the Senate Finance Committee, which oversees major tax, Medicare, Medicaid, Social Security, and trade legislation. He is a member and former chairman of the Senate Commerce, Science and Transportation Committee, and ranking Republican on the Communications Subcommittee. These and other assignments bring his talents to bear on issues as diverse as ocean resource management, economic development, consumer product safety, and foreign commerce.

Packwood's horizons may have expanded to encompass much of the world, but he remains an Oregonian to the core. So what do you get when you combine a state rich in prime cattle ranches with a senator known for his intense love for the outdoors? BARBECUE, of course ...Oregon style.

Barbecue Beef with Northwest Harvest Relish

BARBECUE BEEF WITH NORTHWEST HARVEST RELISH

1 cup commercial chile sauce
1/4 cup fresh lemon juice . . .

Combine the chile sauce, lemon juice, wine, onion, green bell pepper, brown sugar, Worcestershire sauce, jalapeño chile, mustard and minced garlic in a saucepan. Gently simmer over medium-high heat for 10 minutes; remove from heat and cool.

Coat the flank steak strips with the cooled sauce and then grill them quickly over hot coals for 5 to 7 minutes, turning once. Divide the meat strips evenly between the 6 rolls, then top each serving with a portion of the Northwest Harvest Relish.

1/4 cup dry red wine

3 tablespoons each: finely minced onion, green sweet bell pepper

1 tablespoon brown sugar

2 teaspoons Worcestershire sauce

1 jalapeño chile, seeded and minced

1 teaspoon stone-ground mustard

1 clove garlic, minced

1-1/2 pounds flank steak, cut across the grain into long strips measuring not more than 1/2-inch thick (any strips that are longer than 9 inches should be halved)

6 French or Italian rolls, split and toasted

Blanch the uncooked kernels of corn in 2 or 3 cups of boiling water for 30 seconds. Drain, then plunge into cold water to stop the cooking; drain again.

Combine the drained corn and all of the other ingredients in a bowl, and mix well. Adjust the seasonings, adding more salt, pepper, vinegar and oil to taste. Yields about 3 cups relish.

NORTHWEST HARVEST RELISH

1 large uncooked ear of corn, shaved (or 1/2 cup frozen)

1 large tomato, peeled, seeded and diced

1 roasted, seeded and chopped cucumber

1/4 Walla Walla Sweet onion, chopped (if not available, use another sweet Spanish onion variety)

1/4 cup chopped red sweet bell pepper

1/4 cup minced celery

1 jalapeño pepper, seeded and minced

1/4 cup each: wine vinegar and salad oil

2 tablespoons minced parsley

1 tablespoon minced elephant garlic (or 1 large clove regular-size garlic)

Salt and freshly ground black pepper to taste

THE STEINFELD FAMILY

When Henry and Barbara Steinfeld began selling their homemade pickles and sauerkraut door-to-door in 1920, it was to get themselves through an economic disaster in the poultry industry. Bills had to be paid and peddling pickles seemed the best solution at the time. There was no illusion of pursuing a dream.

However, it was obvious from the very beginning that the Steinfelds knew the most important part of the pickle business: how to make good pickles and sauerkraut. So their operation began to grow, and in no time they were able to open a stall at the Portland Farmer's Market. It was certainly easier on their feet, and an even larger though just as neighborly clientele of pickle lovers was established.

Within five years they were using tons of cucumbers and cabbage just to keep up with demand. Land was leased near the Columbia River and bunkhouses built to house the laborers they needed during the harvest. When the Seattle and Spokane markets looked promising, they obtained a Mack truck and began hauling barrels of product to those areas. That's how the business grew. The Steinfeld's sons, Vic and Ray, took over the business during World War II, and, over the next 40 years, built it into the region's finest pickle packing operation. Now a third generation of family is at the helm. Ray's son Ray Jr. is chief executive officer. Vic's son Richard is president, and his daughter, Jane Thomas, is vice president of administration. Ray Sr.'s second son Jim is the chief operating officer.

These days their products are distributed in 11 western states, western provinces of Canada, and Japan. This keeps a lot of Oregon growers happy. For the sauerkraut-making operation alone, about 18 million pounds of cabbage are needed each fall to create the stuff of which Octoberfest dreams are made.

This recipe was developed for Steinfeld's Products by Nancy Strope, Food Editor for Portland's *This Week* magazine. Reuben sandwiches are an epicurean delight when made with Strope's homemade Rye Beer Bread, and the right sauerkraut. It's easy to do if you have a food processor.

Steinfeld's Epicurean Reuben Sandwich

Combine sauerkraut, celery, bell pepper and pimiento. In another bowl, blend together the mayonnaise and chile sauce to make a Thousand Island dressing.

Butter all 8 slices of bread on both sides, then spread 4 slices with the Thousand Island Dressing. Top each slice with about 5 ounces corned beef. Drain the sauerkraut mixture and divide equally between the 4 sandwiches. Add a slice of Swiss cheese to each, then top the sandwiches with the remaining slices of buttered bread.

Grill the sandwiches over medium heat until the cheese has melted and the exterior is golden brown on each side. Serve hot.

STEINFELD'S EPICUREAN REUBEN
*   SANDWICH*
1 (8 ounce) can Steinfeld's Sauerkraut,
*   drained*
1/4 cup finely diced celery
1/4 cup minced green sweet bell pepper
2 tablespoons diced pimiento, well
*   drained*
1/3 cup mayonnaise
1/3 cup chile sauce
8 slices Rye Beer Bread (recipe follows),
*   or a commercial rye or pumpernickel*
1-1/4 pound cooked corned beef
1/2 cup butter or margarine
4 slices Swiss cheese

RYE BEER BREAD

2 cups unsifted unbleached flour

2/3 cup unsifted rye flour

1 tablespoon dark brown sugar

4 teaspoons caraway seed

3/4 teaspoon salt

1 (1/4-ounce) envelope dry yeast

1 cup beer, warmed to 115°

2 tablespoons oil

Place 1 cup of the unbleached flour and all remaining dry ingredients in a food processor; process for approximately 2 seconds.

Mix the warm beer and oil together and add to the dry ingredients, blending until well-mixed. Gradually add the remaining cup of flour, then continue to blend until well mixed and the dough leaves the sides of the processor bowl. Dough will be tacky to the touch. If you use a mixer to make the bread, let the dough mix 8 minutes before adding the final cup of flour. Then continue mixing for 4 more minutes.

Lightly butter hands before handling the dough, then shape the dough into a loaf and place in a buttered 8-1/2 by 4-1/2 by 3-inch bread pan. Butter the surface of the loaf. Cover lightly with a cloth and set to rise in a warm place until the top of the loaf begins to peak over the edge of the pan; about 45 to 50 minutes.

Bake loaf in a 350° oven for 30 minutes, or until loaf sounds hollow when tapped on the bottom with your finger. Allow to cool 10 minutes before slicing.

GOVERNOR NEIL GOLDSCHMIDT

He's been Governor of the State of Oregon, Mayor of Portland, U.S. Secretary of Transportation, and an executive officer for Nike Corporation. If that isn't eclectic enough for you, consider Neil Goldschmidt's youth: choker-setter in the logging industry; graduate of the University of Oregon, where he was president of the student body; summer resident in an Israeli kibbutz; intern for U.S. Senator Maurine Neuberger; voter registration activist in Mississippi during the summer of 1964; and graduate of the University of California's Boalt Law School in 1967.

In 1970 he was elected to the Portland City Council, which ultimately led to two terms as Mayor of Portland, beginning in 1972. During those Mayor Goldschmidt years, Portland inaugurated a national model for mass transit, including a light rail system and downtown transit mall, and revitalized the housing and business in its aging core area.

As Governor, Goldschmidt has presided over the startling recovery of the Oregon economy, and has tried to make state government more responsive to those it is supposed to serve. The Citizen's Representative Office he inherited has been expanded from a three-person operation to a sizzling staff of about 18 people, trained to respond to citizens calling in on toll-free lines for help in dealing with state agencies. He has pushed hard to make progress on matters related to law enforcement and education, challenging decision-makers and the public to face up to the need to make some hard decisions. His own willingness to accept political risks for the sake of doing what he thinks is right for the state may just provide the inspiration they need.

Goldschmidt is in his element when there are children visiting the capitol building, or when he's visiting them in their schools. In fact, children's issues have been his top priority since he took office. It may come as no surprise, then, that this governor's favorite sandwich is a hotdog roll-up. That may not sound very stately or glamorous, but it tracks for a man who enjoys reading Dr. Suess. However, as a nod to dignity, I decided to send this sandwich uptown for some style. Hence the use of puff pastry dough, fine quality sausage, and a well-aged Cheddar cheese.

The Goldschmidt Wrap

THE GOLDSCHMIDT WRAP

*1 pound good-quality smoked
   sausage (I used a nice beef variety but many others, from Cajun
   to Polish, would do as well)*

*2 cups shredded medium or sharp
   Cheddar cheese*

*1 sheet frozen puff pastry, thawed
   and rolled to a rectangle measuring 12 by 14 inches (reserve second sheet for another use)*

Dice the sausage into 1/4-inch pieces. Cut the pastry sheet into 4 rectangles, measuring 6 by 7 inches each. Lay a quarter of the diced sausage, then 1/2 cup of the shredded cheese, down the center of each pastry rectangle. Brush the sides with water, then seal each by bringing the longest edges together in the center and folding over to seal, then fold about an inch of each end toward the center, pressing down to seal. Turn the pouch over so the seam-side faces down and place on a lightly greased baking sheet. Bake in a 425° oven until puffed and golden, about 15 minutes. Yields 4 servings.

RALPH MILLER

Tucson, Ariz.—It ended in the desert on an 88-degree afternoon, the kind Ralph Miller will enjoy at Black Butte and on his scheduled golfing excursions to San Diego, Phoenix and the Caribbean.

It ended with the Oregon State University coach scolding players right into the closing seconds, correcting them, telling them how to do it better next time.

It ended on a 25-foot shot that went in and a 20-footer that didn't—the kind of excitement that might have given a lesser 70-year-old a heart attack.

And it ended—for a crusty old coach nicknamed Whiskey Sour—with nary a dry eye in the room.

Roy Gault, Sports Editor
Corvallis *Gazette-Times*
March 18, 1989

Of the thousands of words written about Ralph Miller's final hours as one of the nation's most respected coaches, Roy Gault's were the most poignant. Yet, Ralph's wife Jean says they were not words she could bear to read at the time. "It was just too painful to dwell on," she said. And the lump still builds inside her throat when she reflects on that final season and the outpouring of love and accolades that surrounded the team—even on opposing teams' courts—after Coach Miller announced his retirement.

Few coaches have received the kind of recognition and respect Coach Miller enjoyed throughout his 38 years as a college basketball coach. But then, few have approached his level of accomplishment. Prior to his 19 seasons at OSU, Miller had six outstanding seasons at the University of Iowa (1964 to 1970), and 13 at Wichita State (1951 to 1964). He managed to win conference championships at all three universities, and was honored in both 1981 and 1982 as national coach of the year. Over the years, Miller produced some of the nation's most explosive offenses, such as Iowa's 1970 squad that averaged over 100 points per game. His Beaver defenses were consistently among the toughest to score against, particularly in the last six years, when they were among the nation's Top 10. When he finally hung up his whistle, he was the sixth winningest college coach of all time.

Miller often observed that the game of basketball hasn't really changed much since its golden era in the 40's, except for the fact that there are now better athletes. However, most maintain that it was the Miller system—Pressure Basketball—that made such efficient use of well-trained athletes. As former USC coach Stan Morrison once commented, "You don't try to beat Miller's players as much as you have to beat Miller's system." That sentiment is consistent with the fact that "blue-chip" recruits were few and far between on Miller teams, and makes his 1987 induction into the Naismith Basketball Hall of Fame all the more appropriate.

When creating the Miller sandwich, I had plenty of help from OSU fans familiar with this popular curmudgeon's personality. Sauerkraut was the most frequently suggested ingredient. Even Jean agreed it would be appropriate, since the Reuben sandwich happens to be one of his favorites. However, at the risk of offending his illustrious arch-rivals to the south, the University of Oregon Ducks, I couldn't help but incorporate Miller's renowned style of play into what will now be considered de rigueur in Miller cuisine—pressed duck.

The Pressed Duck Special

THE PRESSED DUCK SPECIAL

1 (4-1/2 to 5 pound) duckling

1 tablespoon oil

1/3 cup dry sherry

1/3 cup water

3 teaspoons cream-style horseradish

3 teaspoons stoneground mustard

1/2 teaspoon salt

1/2 cup finely minced green onion

2 tablespoons toasted sesame seeds

4 crusty French rolls, split and toasted

1/3 cup mayonnaise

2 tomatoes, thinly sliced

*Heaping cup of shredded mixed romaine
   and iceberg lettuce*

Remove duckling from wrapping; remove giblets (discard or freeze for another use). Salt and pepper outer surface and inside cavity of duckling. Heat the oil in a large, heavy pan, such as a Dutch oven. Place duckling in the pan, breast-side down, and brown over medium-high heat. Turn duckling over and brown back, then remove from heat, cover pan and place in 325° oven. Bake until duckling tests done (30 minutes per pound). Juices will run clear and the meat will be very tender. Remove from oven and allow to cool briefly. When cool enough to handle, remove duckling to cutting board. Drain off all fat from the pan, then deglaze the pan by adding the sherry and water and cooking over medium-high heat, scraping the bottom and sides of pan to remove all of the cooked-on pieces of meat. This creates a flavorful broth. Simmer for about 3 minutes, then remove from heat and stir in 2 teaspoons of the horseradish, 2 teaspoons of the mustard and the salt.

Meanwhile, pick all of the meat off the duckling, discarding skin and bones. With serrated knife or fork, shred the meat into 1- to 1-1/2-inch strips and chunks. You will have about 3 cups of meat. Toss the green onions and sesame seeds with the meat to mix thoroughly, then add the mixture to the pan with the broth and combine well.

Line a 9- by 5-inch loaf pan with a piece of plastic wrap that is large enough to hang out over the sides, then place the mixture in the pan, packing well and evening off the top with a rubber spatula.

Now for the "Pressed Duck" part. Place a second piece of plastic wrap on top of the meat mixture and nest a second 9- by 5-inch loaf pan inside the first pan, so that it rests on top of the meat mixture. In order to actually press the mixture into a compact loaf, load the top loaf pan with 3 pounds of canned goods from your cupboard. Refrigerate this way for 4 to 24 hours.

When ready to assemble sandwiches, remove the top loaf pan and gently lift the duck loaf out of the bottom pan using the plastic wrap for handles. Place on a cutting board and with a sharp knife, cut into 4 rectangles. If necessary, trim the ends of the French rolls to match the length of the duck loaf rectangles. Combine remaining 1 teaspoon of horseradish and mustard with the mayonnaise and spread both sides of each roll with some of the mixture. On lower half, place one of the pieces of duck loaf. Add tomato slices and some of the shredded lettuce, then top with second slice of bread. Yields 4 servings.

If duckling isn't available, a roasting chicken can be substituted. But you couldn't call that a Pressed Duck Special, now could you?

Chapter 4

*T*raditional Twists

As a little girl on a very long road trip with my family one summer, my senses were awakened to the bacon, lettuce, and tomato sandwich. At every lunch spot between San Francisco and Los Angeles, including two days at Disneyland where hamburgers and foot-long hotdogs abound, nothing less than a BLT would do for me.

The experience didn't weary me of this wonderful marriage of flavor and texture. Indeed, the melding is impossible to improve upon, especially when the tomatoes have come straight from a summer garden, as I discovered just a few years ago.

It was after a 12-hour non-stop drive from Oregon to California with my two young nephews. My sister-in-law's mother welcomed us with open arms and freshly made BLT's. Lee had toasted the wholegrained bread to perfection, slathered on a silky layer of mayonnaise, and added thin, tender sheets of lettuce, crisp ribbons of bacon, and thick slices of juicy tomato still warm from the sun. At the moment she thrust this miracle into my hands, a BLT was the farthest thing from my mind. And yet, with the first bite, it turned out to be exactly the right tonic to revive a very weary road warrior. I relish the pleasure of devouring it to this very day.

Such is the way with masterpieces of the sandwich genre. Not flash-in-the pan concoctions, mind you, but items of substance. Culinary couplings of ingredients, that, when combined, do more than occupy the same space in your mouth. Combinations in which the whole is far more sublime than the sum of the parts. You know them by name: Reuben, Club, Chicken Salad, and Grilled Cheese—to mention only a few. On the pages that follow, I've taken some of these great traditions and added just a twist. Not to improve on the originals, but simply to play off their best features.

Fried Egg Sandwich

I was driving our youngest son and a friend to soccer practice one afternoon. Fred had just returned from Boy Scout camp, so when he boarded the van I asked him about the experience. It was great, he said, but then his big brown eyes clouded over and he added, "But you know, it's the grossest thing. They made us eat fried egg sandwiches. Man, can you imagine?"

I locked eyes with my son in the rearview mirror. He was grinning back at my reflection, no doubt thinking about the wonderful fried egg sandwiches we'd had for dinner just the night before.

Fried egg sandwiches. You love 'em or you hate 'em.

We love 'em.

Our family prefers to eat them on soft bread, but you might try toasting it first. It adds extra flavor and texture. Spread both slices with a little mayonnaise and ketchup.

Fry eggs in a skillet, carefully turning them once. Do not break the yolks at this point. After the eggs have been flipped and the white has had a chance to thoroughly set, break the yolks and allow them to run evenly over the eggs. After yolk has set on bottom, flip the eggs again and finish cooking the yolk.

Remove from heat and arrange the eggs on one of the prepared bread slices. Top with the other and serve. Yields 1 serving.

FRIED EGG SANDWICH

2 slices white or whole wheat bread

Mayonnaise

Ketchup

2 eggs

Turkey Club Sandwich

Spread all 12 slices of toasted bread with Thousand Island dressing. Layer 4 of the slices with turkey, avocado, and bacon. Place another slice of toast on top of the bacon, then continue layering each sandwich with tomato slices, cheese, another slice of turkey, hard-cooked eggs and alfalfa sprouts. Top the 4 sandwiches with the remaining 4 slices of bread. Anchor each half with a decorated toothpick or bamboo skewer, then cut the sandwiches in half diagonally. Yields 4 servings.

TURKEY CLUB SANDWICH

12 slices white, whole wheat or
*   pumpernickel bread, toasted*

Thousand Island dressing (commercially
*   bottled, or homemade)*

Sliced turkey

1 avocado, sliced

8 slices cooked bacon

1 tomato, thinly sliced

4 slices Cheddar cheese

2 hard-cooked eggs, sliced

Alfalfa sprouts

Grilled Cheese Sandwich with Pepperoncini

GRILLED CHEESE SANDWICH WITH PEPPERONCINI

8 slices whole grain or whole wheat bread

8 1/4-inch thick slices Cheddar cheese

Greek pepperoncini (slice stem end from each pepper and drain juice)

1/3 cup oil pack sun-dried tomatoes, drained

8 1/4-inch thick slices mild Muenster cheese

Softened butter or margarine

Layer the Cheddar cheese on 4 slices of bread, followed by the pepperoncini, tomatoes, and Muenster cheese. Complete each sandwich with a second slice of bread. Grill the sandwiches in a little butter until they are nicely browned and the cheese melts, turning once after lightly buttering the tops. Yields 4 servings

Towle's Friday Special
(CLOAK AND DAGGER VERSION)

Like many mother/daughter teams, Mom and I shop well together. Even our appetites seem to be in synch. When our psyches begin to droop and not even the sale dresses look good, we know it's time for lunch. It's always been this way, even when I was growing up. Those days, if we were in downtown Burlingame when hunger struck we'd head to our favorite little café on the corner of Burlingame Avenue and Primrose and order the Towle's special.

That was a long time ago, but they're still making it. I sent my mother and sister-in-law back for the recipe, but, as the perennial Friday Special, it remains classified. Not to be deterred, my agents ate $20 worth of sandwiches during two visits, and sleuthed out the essentials for themselves. Their report, plus my photographic palate, and a few slight modifications, went into this recipe.

In a small bowl, combine the tomatoes, olives, parsley, and onions. Stir in enough of the mayonnaise to bind the mixture, but don't make it too soupy.

Cut the slices of cheese to fit the bread. Layer each of 4 bread slices with 1 slice of cheese, 1/4 of the filling, and another slice of cheese. Top each of these with the final 4 slices of bread.

Grill the sandwiches in a little butter until they are nicely browned and the cheese melts, turning once after lightly buttering the tops. Remove sandwiches from heat, cut on the diagonal and serve immediately. Yields 4 servings.

TOWLE'S FRIDAY SPECIAL
(CLOAK AND DAGGER VERSION)

1 cup diced tomato

1 (2-1/4 ounce) can chopped olives, well drained

1 heaping tablespoon each: minced parsley; minced onion

1/4 cup mayonnaise

8 slices mild Cheddar or Monterey Jack cheese (actually, the Towle's version is made with American cheese, so if that's what you prefer, be my guest).

8 slices whole wheat or white bread

Grilled Cheese in French Toast

In a shallow bowl, combine eggs, milk, sherry and Worcestershire. Assemble 4 cheese sandwiches, then dip each in the egg mixture and grill slowly in butter, turning once to get both sides golden brown. Yields 4 servings.

GRILLED CHEESE IN FRENCH TOAST

2 eggs, beaten

1/4 cup milk

1/4 cup dry sherry

1/4 teaspoon Worcestershire sauce

8 slices white or whole wheat bread

4 thick slices Cheddar or Monterey Jack cheese

Almost–Reuben Sandwich

The original Reuben—a grilled masterpiece of cheese, corned beef, sauerkraut and Thousand Island dressing—was created by a cook in an Omaha, Nebraska restaurant. His creation took first place in the 1956 National Sandwich Idea Contest and was an instant national hit.

ALMOST-REUBEN SANDWICH

3 cups chopped corned beef brisket
1 cup sauerkraut, drained and rinsed
1/3 cup finely chopped onion
1/2 cup Thousand Island dressing; more
*   as needed to reach desired consistency*
12 slices pumpernickel bread
12 thin slices of Swiss cheese

Combine corned beef, sauerkraut and onion in a small bowl. Stir in Thousand Island dressing.

Layer each of 6 slices of bread with 1 slice of cheese and a portion of the corned beef mixture. Top with another slice of cheese and a second slice of bread.

Grill the sandwiches in a little butter until they are nicely browned and the cheese melts, turning once after lightly buttering the tops. Yields 6 servings.

Turkey & Stuffing Sandwich

This is the way my mother taught me to eat leftover turkey. The dressing really is a wonderful touch.

TURKEY & STUFFING SANDWICH

2 slices white or whole wheat bread
Mayonnaise
Several slices cooked turkey
About 1/3 cup left-over turkey stuffing
*   (chilled or heated)*

Spread both slices of bread with mayonnaise. Place turkey slices on bottom slice of bread. Add stuffing and top with second slice of bread. An optional ingredient would be cranberry sauce.

Barbecued Chicken Salad with Pine Nuts

Combine oil, soy sauce, bourbon, brown sugar, maple syrup, green onion and garlic; mix well. Add chicken breasts and marinate in the refrigerator for 2 to 4 hours. Grill marinated breasts over medium-hot coals, about 4 minutes per side, brushing the breasts with the marinade as they cook.

Remove from heat and cool thoroughly. Dice chicken into 1/4- to 1/2-inch pieces. Combine with celery, pine nuts, apple, and sweet red or white onion. Stir in enough mayonnaise to thoroughly moisten the ingredients.

To assemble sandwiches, spread each slice of bread with a small amount of mayonnaise. Divide the chicken mixture between 4 of the slices, add lettuce and sprouts, and top with second slice of bread. Cut each sandwich diagonally before serving. Yields 4 servings.

BARBECUED CHICKEN SALAD
*   WITH PINE NUTS*

1/4 cup vegetable oil

1/4 cup soy sauce

1/4 cup bourbon

2 tablespoons brown sugar

2 tablespoons maple syrup

1/4 cup minced green onion

3 cloves garlic, minced

5 or 6 boned and skinned chicken breast
*   halves*

1 cup minced celery

1/2 cup toasted pine nuts

1/2 cup peeled and chopped tart apple

1/4 cup minced sweet red or white onion

About 3/4 cup mayonnaise

8 slices whole grain bread (commercial
*   brand, or use 7-Grain Squaw Bread,*
*   page 161)*

Romaine lettuce leaves

Alfalfa sprouts (or "spicy sprout" mix-
*   ture of alfalfa, radish and cabbage)*

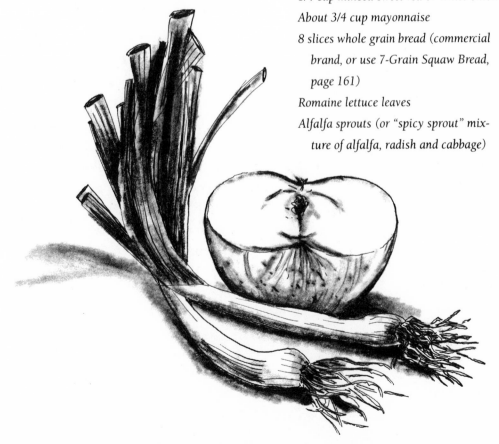

Just-a-Tuna Sandwich. . .

... with dill, that is. It's a surprisingly nice touch.

In a small bowl, combine tuna, enough mayonnaise to moisten it (about 1/4 cup), the dill weed and Worcester-shire sauce. Spread mixture on 3 of the slices of bread, add lettuce and pickles, if desired, then top with second piece of bread. Yields 3 servings.

JUST-A-TUNA SANDWICH ...

Chunk tuna, drained
Mayonnaise to taste
1 teaspoon dried dill weed
1/2 teaspoon Worcestershire sauce
6 slices white or whole wheat bread,
 toasted
Lettuce and pickle slices for garnish,

The Willie Special

Peanut butter sandwiches have always been a very serious matter where my father is concerned. If you ask him how to construct one, you'll get a thorough response:

"Well, first I put the peanut butter on. And then I add a thin slice of red sweet onion—that's RED SWEET onion—and a couple pieces of lettuce. That's really good.

"Or, you can go with just peanut butter and slices of banana. But you have to slice the banana lengthwise. Those are good too.

"Of course, there's also peanut butter and thinly-sliced orange, with a leaf of lettuce if you want. But the lettuce is entirely optional."

See what I mean? Very serious stuff.

The interesting thing is that he isn't alone. Lots of people like lots of things besides honey, jam, or jelly on their peanut butter sandwiches. I've heard of bacon, apples, sunflower seeds, even tomatoes and pickles, for Heaven's sake. So to come up with a unique twist on the tradition-al PB&J would be quite a trick.

What follows is simply a variation of one of my father's favorites, the peanut butter and banana sandwich. However, in this version the bananas are IN the bread as well as ON the peanut butter.

Spread all eight slices of banana bread with peanut butter. Distribute the banana slices evenly among four of the slices, then top with the remaining 4 slices of banana bread. Yields 2 to 4 servings.

THE WILLIE SPECIAL

8 (1/2-inch thick) slices Banana Bread
  (recipe follows)
Peanut butter
1 banana, peeled and cut diagonally into
  1/4-inch thick slices

Cream together butter and sugar. Add eggs and beat well. Combine the flour, salt, and baking soda and stir into the creamed mixture alternately with the mashed bananas. Fold in nuts. Pour batter into greased 9- by 5-inch loaf pan. Bake in 350° oven until a skewer poked into loaf comes out clean, about 45 minutes to 1 hour.

BANANA BREAD

1/2 cup butter
1 cup brown sugar
2 eggs
2 cups all-purpose flour
1/2 teaspoon salt
1/2 teaspoon baking soda
1-1/2 cups mashed bananas
1/2 cup chopped walnuts

Chicken Salad in Sesame & Poppy Seed Vinaigrette with Sugar-Glazed Almonds

This is a delectable twist on the traditional chicken sandwich. It's almost like eating a luscious spinach salad between bread. The Sesame and Poppy Seed Vinaigrette really makes the recipe, so don't substitute with anything else!

CHICKEN SALAD IN SESAME & POPPYSEED VINAIGRETTE WITH SUGAR-GLAZED ALMONDS

4 skinned and boned chicken breast halves, mesquite-grilled

1/2 cup Sesame &Poppy Seed Vinaigrette, Creamy Version (page 170)

1 cup shredded fresh, young spinach leaves (or a combination of young spinach and young dandelion)

2 Roma (Italian-plum) tomatoes, diced

1/2 cup Sugar-Glazed Almonds (recipe follows)

1/4 cup minced red onion

2 hard-cooked eggs, sliced

Salt and pepper to taste

8 slices whole wheat, white or French bread (toasted if desired)

4 leaves romaine lettuce

Cut the cooled pieces of chicken into 1/4-inch pieces and combine with vinaigrette, spinach leaves, tomatoes, almonds and onion. Add more vinaigrette as necessary to reach desired consistency. Salt and pepper to taste.

To assemble sandwiches, spread each of the bread slices with some of the remaining vinaigrette. Divide the chicken mixture evenly between 4 of the slices, then top each with a portion of the egg slices, a leaf of romaine lettuce, and a second slice of bread. Cut diagonally and serve. Yields 4 servings.

It's not necessary to grill the chicken over mesquite coals, but it does impart a wonderful flavor. They can be grilled up to 24 hours ahead and refrigerated until ready to assemble the salad mixture. Alternately, you can simply grill the boneless, skinless chicken breasts in the oven, turning once and cooking until done.

In non-stick skillet (or skillet sprayed with non-stick vegetable spray), roast 1/2 cup sliced almonds over medium-high heat until golden, shaking the pan to prevent scorching. Once the almonds have browned, sprinkle on the sugar, stirring constantly, and cook until the sugar melts around the almonds. Remove from heat and quickly scrape the almonds onto a sheet of waxed paper to cool. Yields 1/2 cup almonds.

SUGAR-GLAZED ALMONDS

1/2 cup sliced almonds
2 to 3 teaspoons granulated sugar

MENUS

ANYTIME FRIDAY SPECIAL

A Consommé of Beef with Sherry
And Garlic Butter Croutons (page 162)

Towle's Friday Special (page 83)
Tossed Green Salad with Italian Dressing,
Marinated Artichoke Hearts, and Mushroom Slices

Hazelnut Wafers (page 174)

A SPRING SUPPER

Cabbage Salad
With Yellow and Red Sweet Bell Peppers

Barbecued Chicken Salad with Pine Nuts (page 85)
Chilled Asparagus Spears
With Sesame Mayonnaise (page 28)

Strawberries with Sweet Cream

Chapter 5

Open-Face Sandwiches

I've always enjoyed the open-face sandwich concept, for one reason or another. In my early years when anything more exotic than hamburger was disdained, I appreciated their openness, allowing for easy inspection of the meal. As an adult, I enjoy the respectability factor of the open-face. That is, the ability to legally eat with your fingers and not get sent to your room, even if you really make a mess.

And finally, as a mother, I have come to appreciate how easily open-face sandwiches become a meal. Starting with a base of carbohydrate—loosely defined as bread, but more realistically incorporating anything from cracker to muffin—I can usually cull at least half a dozen likely topping candidates from pantry and fridge. Then it's dinner, and on to the soccer game.

Egg-in-Your-Face

EGG-IN-YOUR-FACE

4 slices whole wheat bread, toasted

Mayonnaise

Dijon mustard

4 thin slices ham

8 thin slices ripe tomato

Egg Salad Louie! Louie! (page 155)

1 ripe avocado, peeled and sliced
  vertically into 1/2-inch thick slices

1/4 cup finely chopped green onion

Spread each slice of bread with a little mayonnaise and mustard, then layer each with 2 tomato slices and one fourth of the egg salad. Arrange one fourth of the avocado slices attractively on each sandwich, then sprinkle with about 1 tablespoon of onion. Yields 4 servings.

Chicken & Tomato Baguettes

CHICKEN & TOMATO BAGUETTES

3/4 cup mayonnaise

1/2 cup chopped green onions

1/2 cup toasted hazelnuts, chopped

1 tablespoon Dijon mustard

1 teaspoon Worcestershire sauce

1 teaspoon salt

Several dashes hot pepper sauce

4 chicken breast halves, skinned, boned,
  poached and chopped

2 cups shredded fontina cheese and 1
  cup shredded Monterey Jack cheese,
  combined

1 baguette French bread

1 cup chopped tomato

1 tablespoon fresh chopped basil

Sliced green onions, parsley, and sliced
  olives for garnishes

In a large bowl, combine mayonnaise, green onions, hazelnuts, mustard, Worcestershire, salt and hot pepper sauce. Stir in chicken and half of the cheese. This mixture can be stored covered in the refrigerator for up to 24 hours before use.

Slice baguette lengthwise, and place halves face up on a baking sheet. Stir tomato and basil into chicken mixture. Spread evenly over each bread half and sprinkle with remaining cheese. Bake about 10 minutes at 400°, until cheese is bubbly and lightly browned. Transfer to a long cutting board prior to garnishing with parsley, sliced green onions, or olives. Slice and serve. Yields 6 servings.

Matilda's Quickie

This creation won John Heggen of Corvallis the Grand Prize in the Corvallis *Gazette-Times* 1986 recipe contest, "Northwest Cooks." It's so amazingly simple that most people were surprised by its success. But if you try it, you'll understand how it carried the day.

Combine the chile with the mayonnaise and set aside. Lay the bread on a cookie sheet and top with the slices of cheese. Lay the tomato slices on top of the cheese, then spread with the mayonnaise mixture. Add a dash of oregano. Broil in oven until cheese and mayonnaise are bubbly. Serve whole, or cut each portion in half. Yields 4 servings.

For a lively garnish, top each portion with a thin slice of jalapeño chile.

MATILDA'S QUICKIE

1 small green chile, such as a jalapeño, finely minced
1/3 cup mayonnaise
4 slices bread
4 large slices Cheddar cheese
2 tomatoes, sliced
Oregano

Tuna Melt with Avocado

In a bowl, combine tuna, dressing, celery, green onion, and pepper. Divide mixture between the 8 English muffin halves. Top each sandwich with some avocado and then the cheeses. Place sandwiches on baking sheet and broil until toppings are hot and bubbly. Yields 4 servings.

TUNA MELT WITH AVOCADO

1 (12-1/2 ounce) can water-pack alba-core tuna, drained and flaked
1/2 cup Italian dressing
1 cup chopped celery
1/2 cup chopped green onion
1/2 cup chopped green sweet bell pepper
4 English muffins, split and toasted
2 avocados, peeled, pitted and cut cross-wise into 1/2-inch thick slices
1-1/2 cups shredded fontina or Swiss cheese

Sandwich à l'Alsatian

When there is a reference to "Alsatian" in a recipe, it usually means "as done, used, or prepared in Alsace," one of France's eastern provinces. The dish will include ingredients such as sauerkraut, ham, sausage, foie gras, or boiled potatoes.

In a small saucepan, combine tomato sauce, butter, wine vinegar, basil, sugar, salt and pepper. Simmer for 10 minutes.

Meanwhile, spread the 4 bread slices with mustard and place each one on a dinner plate. In a skillet, sauté the sausage over medium heat until browned. Add sauerkraut and continue to sauté just until the sauerkraut is heated through. Place one fourth of this mixture on each of the bread slices; top with the gherkins. Spoon the hot tomato sauce over the sandwiches and serve. Yields 4 servings.

SANDWICH à l'ALSATIAN

1 (16 ounce) can tomato sauce

3 tablespoons butter

2 tablespoons wine vinegar

1 teaspoon dried basil

1 teaspoon sugar

Salt and pepper to taste

4 slices pumpernickel

Dijon mustard

1 pound Polish or Italian sausage,
  sliced into 1/2-inch pieces

1 cup sauerkraut, drained and rinsed

8 or 9 gherkins or baby dills, chopped

Artichoke Broil

Combine artichoke hearts, mayonnaise and Parmesan. Spread one fourth of the mixture on the toasted side of each bread slice. Broil until hot and bubbly. Yields 4 servings.

ARTICHOKE BROIL

1 cup chopped marinated artichoke
  hearts
1/2 cup mayonnaise
1/4 cup grated Parmesan cheese
4 (1/2- to 3/4-inch thick) slices French
  bread, toasted on one side

Baloney Boats

Did you know that when you broil baloney, the sides curl up? Suddenly you have a little round boat. This simple little characteristic of an otherwise humdrum luncheon meat endeared me to baloney at an early age. Try it on your kids and they'll probably be just as happy to gobble down a fleet of Baloney Boats as I was.

Arrange a slice of baloney on each slice of bread. Place on a baking sheet and broil until baloney turns golden brown and the sides curl up into a round "boat" or "bowl." Add a little slice of cheese in the center and continue broiling just until the edges of the bread begin to toast and the cheese begins to melt. Serve with mustard, ketchup and pickles on the side. Yields 2 servings.

BALONEY BOATS

2 slices baloney
2 slices white bread
Cheese
Mustard, ketchup and pickles

Duxelles & Cheese Broil

This is an excellent reason to have a supply of duxelles on hand in your fridge at all times!

Arrange the English muffins face up on a baking sheet and broil until golden brown; remove from oven.

In a small bowl, combine the duxelles and shredded Cheddar cheese. Spread one-eighth of the mixture on each of the muffin halves, then return the baking sheet to the oven and broil until mixture is hot and bubbly.

Remove sandwiches from oven, then top each with some of the tomatoes, a generous dollop of sour cream, and a sprinkling of Parmesan. Serve immediately. Yields 4 servings.

DUXELLES & CHEESE BROIL

4 English muffins, split
1 cup duxelles (page 168)
1 cup shredded medium Cheddar cheese
1-1/2 cups diced tomatoes
*Sour cream and grated Parmesan cheese
   for garnish*

Ham & Vegetables in Velouté

In a saucepan, melt the butter over medium heat. With a wire whisk, blend in the flour, and stir the mixture over moderately low heat for 2 minutes. Remove pan from heat and whisk in the chicken broth in a steady stream. Return pan to the burner and cook over medium-high heat, stirring constantly, for 5 minutes or until thickened. Stir in the scalded heavy cream, then remove pan from heat. You will have about 2 cups of velouté. If not using the sauce immediately, let it cool for about 4 minutes, then gently smooth a sheet of waxed paper or plastic wrap onto its surface to prevent formation of a skin, and refrigerate.

Peel the broccoli stalks and chop enough stalks and flowerets to yield 2 cups of broccoli pieces. Place the

HAM & VEGETABLES IN VELOUTE

4 tablespoons butter
3 tablespoons flour
1-1/3 cups chicken broth
*1/3 cup scalded heavy cream
   (recipe follows)*
About 1/2 pound broccoli
*1 cup chopped fennel bulb (about 1/2
   medium-sized bulb)*
1 cup chopped yellow onion
2 cups diced ham
*1 jar (6 ounces) marinated artichoke
   hearts, drained and chopped to yield
   1/3 cup*
3/4 cup shredded Cheddar cheese
6 English muffins, split and toasted

broccoli in a steamer rack along with the fennel and onion; cover and steam over rapidly boiling water for about 8 minutes (broccoli will be softened but not completely tender—do not overcook). Place the steamed vegetables, ham, and marinated artichoke hearts in the pan with the sauce (if the sauce was made ahead, gently reheat before adding the vegetables); gently combine. Keep mixture on low heat.

For each serving, place the two halves of an English muffin face up on a dinner plate. Sprinkle each muffin with a portion of the shredded cheese, then spoon on a generous portion of the Vegetables in Velouté. The sauce will just begin to melt the cheese, leaving it slightly firm. Serve immediately. Yields 6 servings.

SCALDED CREAM

The term "scalding" means to heat the cream in a small saucepan over medium-high heat just until tiny bubbles begin to form around the edge. Do not bring the cream to a boil.

Surimi Sandwiches in a Flash

There's plenty to be said for imitation crab. Just be sure you don't try to pass it off as REAL crab. That would be cheating. Besides, you wouldn't fool a soul. This particular sandwich has been friend Sheri Albin's annual Halloween luncheon special for at least 4 years. Nobody in our group wants her to serve anything else. Which is just fine with Sheri because it means she can zoom home from work and have it thrown together in 30 minutes.

SURIMI SANDWICHES IN A FLASH

1-1/2 pounds surimi (imitation crab flakes)

8 green onions, thinly chopped

2 cups salad dressing

2 cups sharp Cheddar cheese, shredded

2 cups medium Cheddar cheese, shredded

Lemon pepper seasoning salt (optional)

8 Kaiser rolls, split

In a large bowl, combine surimi with onions, salad dressing, cheeses and, if desired, lemon pepper seasoning salt. Divide mixture between the 16 Kaiser halves. Broil until cheese is melted and mixture is hot and golden. Yields 8 servings.

MENUS

HARVEST SUPPER

Spinach Salad
With Sesame & Poppy Seed Vinaigrette (page 170)
And Glazed Almonds (page 89)

Duxelles & Cheese Broil (page 96)
Chilled Artichokes
With Lemon & Herb Sauce (page 11)

Summer Blackberry Pie (page 176)

A TANTALIZING MEDLEY

Tossed Green Salad
With Curry Vinaigrette (page 166)

Ham & Vegetables in Velouté (page 96)
Steamed Broccoli with Herbed Butter

Raspberry Sherbet
With Grandma Skinner's Scottish Shortbread (page 178)

Chapter 6

*P*ockets, Roll-Ups, & Wraps

The idea that sandwich architecture is limited to whatever can be confined between two slices of bread is, of course, too confining. But it wasn't so long ago that the phrase "pocket bread" would elicit little more than blank looks from otherwise savvy cooks. These days, everything from cracker bread to tortillas sees duty in sandwich fare. And if you send a youngster to the store for a package of pocket bread, be sure to specify white or whole wheat, plain or sesame, and mealsize or mini.

Pocket Fajitas

POCKET FAJITAS

4-1/2 pound bone-in beef chuck roast

1 (7 ounce) can diced green chiles

1/2 cup mild green taco sauce

3 tablespoons chile powder

1 tablespoon cumin powder

1 teaspoon dried oregano leaves

2 cloves garlic, minced

1 (16 ounce) can stewed tomatoes

Salt to taste

Cayenne pepper to taste

8 pocket breads, halved

*Condiments: guacamole (page 169), sour
    cream, salsa, shredded cheese, shred-
    ded lettuce, pickled jalapeño slices*

Place roast on a 12- by 25-inch sheet of aluminum foil. Mix together green chiles, taco sauce, chile powder, cumin, oregano and garlic. Spread mixture on top of roast, then wrap the foil around the roast and seal. Place roast in a pan and bake in 300° oven for 4 to 4-1/2 hours or until meat is so tender it falls apart. Carefully unwrap roast (the steam is very hot!) and discard fat and bones. Shred meat and put meat and drippings into a large pan. Stir in stewed tomatoes, salt, and cayenne pepper to taste; bring mixture to a boil. Cool slightly and transfer to a serving bowl.

Diners can assemble their own sandwiches by stuffing pocket bread halves with the beef and condiments of their choice. Yields 8 servings.

Exquisite Calzones

EXQUISITE CALZONES

1 (15 ounce) container ricotta cheese

1 cup shredded provolone cheese

1 cup shredded fontina cheese

1/4 pound sliced prosciutto, chopped

*1 (2-1/4 ounce) can sliced olives,
    drained . . .*

When piping hot, these make delicious mid-winter supper fare. Chilled, they travel well to a summer picnic.

In a large bowl, combine ricotta, provolone, and fontina cheeses, prosciutto, olives, pepperoncini, tomatoes and basil; set aside. Brush 2 large baking sheets with olive oil (preferably that drained from the tomatoes) or salad oil; set aside.

Divide each loaf of bread dough into 3 pieces. On a floured surface, roll each piece into a 7-inch round. On half of each round, place a heaping 1/2 cup of the ricotta mixture and spread it to within 1/2 inch of the edge.

In a small bowl, beat the egg with the water. Brush the mixture over edges of dough rounds, then fold empty half of dough round over the filling, forming a crescent shape. Press or decoratively pinch edges to seal.

Place 3 calzones on each baking sheet; brush each calzone with oil and bake in a 400° oven for 30 to 35 minutes, or until golden brown. Serve immediately, or cool, then wrap and refrigerate. Re-warm to desired temperature in a microwave oven prior to serving. Yields 6 servings.

About 10 Greek pepperoncini, stemmed and chopped

1/3 cup chopped sun-dried tomatoes, well drained

2 tablespoons chopped fresh basil leaves (or 2 teaspoons dried)

2 loaves (1 pound each) frozen bread dough, thawed

1 large egg

1 tablespoon water

Salad oil, or olive oil drained from tomatoes

Pocket Delight

A delightful melange of fresh, crunchy vegetables, grated cheese, diced egg and sunflower seeds, all tucked into a chewy pocket of bread, then drizzled with either of two sauces.

In a bowl, combine carrots, celery, cheese, tomatoes, green onions, sunflower seeds, eggs, and avocado, tossing to mix thoroughly. To assemble the sandwiches, diners stuff the pocket halves with a portion of the filling, some alfalfa sprouts, and then drizzle on either one or both of the sauces. Yields 4 servings.

POCKET DELIGHT

1 cup finely chopped carrot

1 cup finely chopped celery

1 cup shredded Cheddar or Monterey Jack cheese

3 tomatoes, cored and diced

1/2 cup finely chopped green onion

1/2 cup shelled sunflower seeds

3 hard-cooked eggs, peeled and chopped

1 or 2 ripe avocados, seeded, peeled and diced

4 pocket breads, halved

Alfalfa sprouts

Raita Sauce (page 168)

Pocket Delight Vinaigrette (page 169)

Sesame Chicken Pockets

SESAME CHICKEN POCKETS

*5 chicken breast halves, skinned and
   boned*

2 tablespoons salad oil

1 teaspoon sesame oil

1-1/2 tablespoons sesame seeds

2 tablespoons red or white wine vinegar

*1 tablespoon each: soy sauce, granulat-
   ed sugar, ketchup*

1 teaspoon Worcestershire sauce

1/2 teaspoon red chile flakes

*1 small jalapeño chile, seeded and finely
   minced*

*1 medium-sized cucumber, peeled, seed-
   ed and diced*

2 medium tomatoes, diced

1 red onion, minced

*1/2 teaspoon dried rosemary (or 1 tea-
   spoon fresh, finely minced)*

4 pocket breads, halved

2 to 3 cups shredded lettuce

2 cups shredded Monterey Jack cheese

1/2 pint sour cream

Dice chicken into 1/2-inch pieces, then sauté in skillet with the oils over medium-high heat until lightly golden. While the chicken is browning, make a well in the center of the pan and add the sesame seeds, gently stirring them occasionally until browned. Add vinegar, soy sauce, sugar, ketchup, Worcestershire, chile flakes, and about half of the jalapeño (add more later if you want to add some zip); set aside, and refrigerate if not to be used within 30 minutes.

About half an hour before serving, combine the cucumber, tomatoes, onions and rosemary. Diners fill pocket halves with the chicken and tomato mixtures, lettuce, and cheese, then garnish with sour cream. Yields 4 servings.

Chicken mixture can be covered and stored in the refrigerator for up to 24 hours. Re-heat at least to room temperature before use.

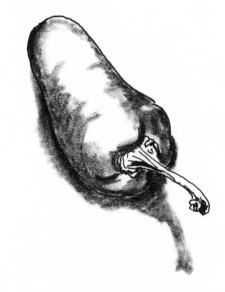

Barbecued Lamb Kabobs with Sautéed Onions in a Pocket

Combine salad dressing, soy sauce and red pepper flakes. Place lamb and onions in a flat-bottomed container or plastic bag and pour the marinade over them. Close container or bag and refrigerate for 4 to 12 hours, turning contents occasionally so they marinate evenly.

When ready to proceed, stack the pocket breads on a sheet of heavy foil and wrap tightly. Warm in a 325° oven for about 10 minutes. In a small bowl, prepare the yogurt sauce by combining the yogurt, mint, and cucumber.

Lift meat from marinade and drain. Thread the meat onto metal or bamboo skewers and place on a lightly greased grill 4 to 6 inches above a solid bed of glowing coals. Cook, turning frequently until lamb is well browned on all sides but still pink in the center when slashed, about 12 to 15 minutes.

Meanwhile, drain onions and sauté them in a skillet over medium-high heat until soft. Using a slotted spoon, transfer onions to a serving bowl. Diners fill pocket bread halves with a handful of mixed greens, 5 or 6 pieces of lamb, sautéed onions, tomatoes, cucumbers, and finish with a dollop of the yogurt sauce. Yields 6 servings.

BARBECUED LAMB KABOBS WITH SAUTEED ONIONS IN A POCKET

1 (8-ounce) bottle herb & garlic salad dressing

1/2 cup soy sauce

1/2 teaspoon red pepper flakes

2 pounds lean boneless lamb (shoulder or leg), cut into 3/4-inch pieces

5 yellow onions, thinly sliced

6 pocket breads

2 cups unflavored yogurt

1/2 cup finely chopped cucumber

2 tablespoons chopped fresh mint

About 3 cups of mixed greens, broken into pieces (a combination of romaine, baby dandelion leaves, radiccio and arugula is nice)

3 medium-sized tomatoes, cut into thin wedges

2 medium-sized cucumbers, thinly sliced

Sub-Jee

During my junior year in college I lived next door to a student visiting from India. On Friday nights, a group of us would often convene in his apartment for a pot of "sub-jee"—really nothing more than a spicy vegetable stew roll-up. Each of us would bring a different vegetable for the pot, which my neighbor diced before tossing in. Then he'd pull half a dozen spices from his cupboard and start adding them to the simmering melange. Pretty soon the apartment would be filled with the zesty aroma of chiles, cumin, cilantro, and coriander.

Once the vegetables reached an advanced stage of fork-tender, he would bring the pot into the living room and set it on a coffee table layered with newspapers. We'd gather around to fill steaming-hot flour tortillas with the exotic mixture, then spoon on some diced fresh tomatoes and generous slatherings of sour cream as cooling counterpoints to the concoction's spicy bite. Then we'd fold the tortillas burrito-style, and gobble our creations out of hand.

SUB-JEE

2 tablespoons olive oil

1/4 pound fresh mushrooms, sliced

1 small head cauliflower, cut into florets

4 medium-sized red or white potatoes

1 cup chopped yellow onion

1 cup sliced celery

1 finely minced jalapeño pepper

2 teaspoons cumin powder

2 teaspoons curry powder . . .

In a large, heavy pot, heat the oil over medium-high heat. Add mushrooms and sauté until they release their juices and begin to brown. Stir in cauliflower, potatoes, onion, celery, jalapeño, cumin, curry, garlic, salt, cayenne, cinnamon and broth. Cover the pot and braise the mixture over medium heat for about 20 minutes, or until vegetables are very tender.

To serve, heat flour tortillas one at a time in a dry skillet until they're soft and pliable, then sprinkle with a little grated Monterey Jack cheese. Have each diner spoon some of the vegetable mixture down the center of a tortilla, then top with diced fresh tomatoes and a dollop of sour cream. To eat, roll the tortilla around the filling, burrito-fashion. Wonderful! Yields 6 to 8 servings.

1 or 2 cloves garlic, minced

1/2 to 1 teaspoon salt

1/4 teaspoon cayenne

Dash cinnamon

3 cups chicken broth

6 to 8 thick flour tortillas

About 2 cups shredded Monterey Jack cheese

3 fresh tomatoes, diced

1 cup sour cream

Pocket Burgers

Cut each pocket bread in half, crosswise. Wrap the halves tightly in foil and warm in 300° oven for about 15 minutes.

Meanwhile, combine the lamb, onion, parsley, cilantro, salt, cumin, paprika and cayenne pepper. Shape the meat mixture into twelve 1/2-inch thick oval patties (shaped to fit the pocket halves). Grill, broil or fry the burgers to desired doneness. To assemble, diners fill each pocket half with a burger, any of the fillings desired, and a generous dollop of the Raita Sauce. Yields 6 servings.

POCKET BURGERS

6 pocket breads

2 pounds ground lamb

1 cup finely chopped yellow onion

1/2 cup finely chopped parsley

1/4 cup finely chopped cilantro

2 teaspoons salt

2 teaspoons cumin powder

1 teaspoon paprika

1/2 teaspoon cayenne pepper

Fillings: sliced red onion, shredded Monterey Jack or Cheddar cheese, crumbled feta cheese, alfalfa sprouts, sliced or diced tomato

Raita Sauce (page 168)

Peking Porkburger Roll-ups

PEKING PORKBURGER ROLL-UPS

1-1/2 pounds lean ground pork

1 medium-sized yellow onion, finely chopped

1/3 cup fine dry bread crumbs

1 egg

1/2 cup finely chopped water chestnuts

2 tablespoons toasted sesame seeds

2 tablespoons soy sauce

1 tablespoon chopped fresh cilantro

1/2 teaspoon ground ginger

8 flour tortillas, 6 to 8 inches in diameter

About 1-1/2 cups shredded Monterey Jack cheese

Peking Sauce (recipe follows)

1 cup chopped green onion

2 cups bean sprouts

PEKING SAUCE

In a bowl, combine pork, onion, bread crumbs, egg, water chestnuts, sesame seeds, soy sauce, cilantro, and ginger. Mix well, then shape into 8 small rolls, each about 4 inches long.

To cook, place the pork rolls on a grill 4 to 6 inches above a solid bed of glowing coals. Cook, turning at least 4 times to brown evenly, for 12 to 14 minutes, or until meat is no longer pink in the middle. If barbecuing is impractical, pork can be broiled 4 to 6 inches below an oven element for 12 to 14 minutes.

To serve, heat each tortilla in a skillet over medium-high heat, turning once. After turning the tortilla, sprinkle the warmed surface with some of the cheese. As soon as cheese begins to melt, transfer tortilla to a platter for someone to begin assembling.

Begin assembly by spreading the tortilla with Peking Sauce. Place a pork roll near one edge edge of the tortilla, then top with some of the green onions and bean sprouts. Fold the edge of the tortilla over filling, fold in tortilla sides and roll up to enclose the filling. Yields 8 servings.

In a small bowl, combine 1/3 cup ketchup, 1/4 cup hoisin sauce (available in Oriental sections of most supermarkets), 2 tablespoons Chinese hot mustard paste, and 1/2 teaspoon sesame oil. Yields 2/3 cup.

Pizza Roll-Up

Pizza in a loaf! With the ingredients on the inside, you have a delicious and unusually tidy pizza.

Dissolve yeast and the 2 teaspoons sugar in the 1/2 cup of lukewarm water; set aside for 5 minutes. In a saucepan, combine 1-1/2 cups water, powdered milk, salt, sugar and olive oil; heat to lukewarm. In a large bowl, add yeast and milk mixtures to flour. Stir until blended and then beat for 3 to 5 minutes. Turn dough out onto a floured board and knead until dough is smooth and elastic, about 10 minutes. Lightly coat a bowl with a little more olive oil and place dough in it, turning to coat all sides. Cover with damp towel and allow to rise in a warm place for 1 hour. Punch down, cover and allow to rise for another hour.

Divide dough into two halves; cover one and set aside. On floured board, roll the other half into a 12- by 14-inch rectangle. Spread with half the pizza filling and, starting from a short end, roll up like a jelly roll. Place seam side down on a greased baking sheet. Repeat with other portion of dough. Cut slits across tops of rolls at 1-inch intervals. Cover with towel and allow to rise for 1/2 hour. Bake in 350° oven for 25 to 35 minutes or until golden brown. When cooked, brush tops with melted butter, sprinkle with Parmesan cheese, and serve. Yields 6 to 8 servings.

In a skillet, cook sausage; drain fat. Add peppers, onions and garlic; cook for 3 more minutes, then remove skillet from heat. Add remaining ingredients to the sausage mixture and mix well.

PIZZA ROLL-UP

2 packages dry yeast

2 teaspoons sugar

1/2 cup lukewarm water (105 to 115°)

1-1/2 cups water

1/4 cup powdered nonfat milk

1-1/2 teaspoons salt

2 tablespoons sugar

1/4 cup olive oil, plus about 1 tablespoon

6 cups all-purpose flour

1/4 cup butter, melted

Pizza filling (recipe follows)

Parmesan Cheese

PIZZA FILLING

1-1/2 pounds bulk Italian sausage

1 green sweet bell pepper, finely chopped

1 medium-sized onion, finely chopped

2 cloves garlic, minced

1/2 pound pepperoni, finely minced in food processor

1/4 pound prosciutto, chopped

1/2 pound shredded mozzarella cheese

1/2 cup grated Parmesan cheese

MENUS

JUST A LITTLE ITALY!

Minestrone Soup with Freshly Grated Parmesan Cheese
Bread Sticks with Spinach Presto Sauce (page 167)

Exquisite Calzones (page 102)
Pasta Salad of Rotelle & Olives
On a bed of Tossed Greens & Vinaigrette

Spumoni Ice Cream

A TEMPTING GRILL

Summer Gazpacho (page 159)
With Grilled Baguette Slices

Pocket Burgers (page 107)
Potato Salad

Timberline Cherry Tart (page 25-26)

Chapter 7

Exciting Entrées

There are days when the task of creating flavorful and diverse meals seems just too much. So you poach some chicken breasts, slap a few boiled potatoes on the table and call it good.

But it's certainly not great, is it? Not by a long shot. Great is color, flavor and texture joining forces in the center of your brain, for a zowie-bow-dow! experience. Great is when unusual and exciting new flavors throw a hoedown on your tongue. The sandwiches in this chapter are ideal for pepping up your menu. Depending on how they are presented, they suffice equally well for a simple family supper or a friendly dinner party. Some can even go formal!

Harvest Thyme Sandwich

This sandwich, created by Mary Lou Newhouse of South Burlington, Vermont, won First Place in the Indoor category of the 1989 National Beef Cook-off®.

HARVEST THYME BEEF SANDWICH

1-1/2 pound boneless beef top sirloin steak, cut 1-1/2 inch thick
Dressing (recipe follows)
4 French rolls, split and lightly toasted
1 cup each: finely shredded carrot, turnip
4 large leaves red leaf lettuce
1/4 cup thinly sliced green onion tops
Thin apple slices dipped in lemon juice
1/4 cup drained prepared horseradish (optional)
Paprika (optional)

Prepare dressing. Trim excess fat from steak. Place steak and 3/4 cup Dressing in plastic bag, turning to coat. Close bag securely and marinate in refrigerator 1 hour, turning occasionally. Place steak on rack in broiler pan so surface of meat is 4 to 5 inches from heat. Broil 25 to 30 minutes for rare to medium, turning once. Carve steak diagonally into thin slices. Place French rolls face up on plates. Mix carrot and turnip together, then layer on one side of each roll. Place one lettuce leaf on other side of each roll; top with beef and green onion. Drizzle remaining dressing not used for marinade over both sides of sandwich. Garnish sandwiches with apple slices. For most dramatic presentation, serve sandwiches open-face. Diners may wish to add horseradish and/or paprika before closing sandwiches. Yields 4 servings.

DRESSING

3/4 cup plus 2 tablespoons extra-virgin olive oil
1/4 cup fresh lemon juice
1/4 cup red wine vinegar
1 tablespoon Bavarian-style mustard, or other strong dark mustard
1 teaspoon salt
3/4 teaspoon crumbled dried thyme leaves
1/2 teaspoon coarsely cracked black pepper

Whisk together olive oil, lemon juice and vinegar. Slowly whisk in mustard until blended. Add salt, thyme and pepper. Yields about 1-1/2 cups.

Grilled Steak Sandwich with Oregon Bleu

Grill flank steak to desired stage of doneness. Meanwhile, combine the bleu cheese, mayonnaise, tomato sauce, olive oil and garlic in a food processor. Blend until smooth, then spread on both halves of each roll.

When steak is cooked, slice into thin strips, across the grain and at a slight angle (to maximize tenderness). Place a fourth of the meat on the bottom half of each roll, then add dollops of the bleu cheese spread on top of the meat. Garnish with onion, sun-dried tomatoes and bell pepper slices. Close sandwiches and serve. Yields 6 servings.

GRILLED STEAK SANDWICH WITH
OREGON BLEU

1-1/2 pound flank steak

3 ounces Oregon Bleu cheese (or Roquefort)

1/3 cup mayonnaise

1 tablespoon tomato sauce

1 tablespoon olive oil (preferably from the jar of sun-dried tomatoes)

1 clove garlic, minced

6 French rolls, split and toasted

1/3 cup sun-dried tomatoes, coarsely chopped

Thin slices of red onion and sweet bell pepper

Leek & Shrimp Supper on a Roll

Spring Leeks and spring Pacific shrimp, two delicate flavors, combine for a powerful sandwich. Use only fresh, or fresh-frozen shrimp. The canned ones simply won't do.

Sauté leeks in olive oil until softened, about 3 minutes. Stir in broth, cream, and white pepper. Simmer until the liquid is reduced and leeks are very tender.

Let mixture cool slightly, then stir in the shrimp and olives. Adjust seasoning, adding salt and additional white pepper to taste. Divide the mixture between the 4 French rolls, garnish with tomatoes and serve. Yields 4 servings.

LEEK & SHRIMP SUPPER
ON A ROLL

4 cups chopped leeks

1 tablespoon olive oil

1/4 cup chicken broth

1/4 cup light cream . . .

1/4 teaspoon white pepper

1/2 pound cooked Pacific shrimp

1/3 cup sliced olives

Salt to taste

4 French rolls, split and toasted

Seasonal garnish: sliced tomatoes
  (only if fresh from a local producer)

Mesquite-Grilled Chicken Salad with Teriyaki Onions

MESQUITE-GRILLED CHICKEN
  SALAD WITH TERIYAKI ONIONS

4 chicken breast halves, skinned and
  boned

4 slices bacon, diced

1 medium-sized onion, finely chopped

2 teaspoons red wine vinegar

1 teaspoon soy sauce

1 teaspoon sugar

1/4 teaspoon ground ginger

About 1/4 cup mayonnaise (more or less
  to taste)

1 cup shredded fontina cheese

4 French rolls, split and toasted

1 avocado, peeled, seeded and sliced

Spicy Sprouts (A mixture of alfalfa,
  radish and cabbage is most common;
  otherwise, just use alfalfa)

Just before preparing the sandwiches, grill the chicken breasts; cool slightly and dice into 3/8-inch pieces.

Meanwhile, sauté bacon over medium-high heat until crisp, then remove to paper towels and drain well. Remove all but 1 tablespoon of the bacon drippings from the pan. Reduce temperature to medium, add chopped onion and sauté until softened, about 3 or 4 minutes. Stir in the vinegar, soy sauce, sugar and ginger and cook until liquid is reduced; remove from heat and cool slightly. In a small bowl, combine the chicken chunks, onion mixture, mayonnaise and shredded cheese. Add additional mayonnaise as needed to reach desired consistency. Divide the mixture evenly between bottom halves of the 4 rolls. Layer on the avocado slices and sprouts. Spread a little mayonnaise on the top halves of the rolls before closing the sandwiches. Yields 4 servings.

Chicken can be grilled and chopped up to 24 hours in advance. Store covered in the refrigerator, and re-warm before using.

Mesquite-Grilled Chicken Sandwich with Gruyère & Sun-Dried Tomatoes

In Portland, Oregon, at the 23rd Street location of Papa Haydn, I enjoyed a salad created by Lunch Chef Deborah Loftus. The chicken mixture is so exotic and unique that I decided to adapt it to a sandwich. Don't skimp on the quality of your bread—this recipe deserves the best. It makes a wonderful luncheon or dinner for special guests.

Grill chicken over mesquite coals; set aside until cool enough to handle.

Dice the chicken breasts into 3/8-inch pieces. In a large bowl, combine the chicken, ham, cheese, bell pepper, sun-dried tomatoes and capers. Toss with the vinaigrette until all ingredients are well coated; chill for at least 30 minutes while flavors blend. Mixture can be made up to 12 hours ahead.

When ready to serve, spread both halves of each roll with the Pesto Mayonnaise. Layer the chicken mixture on the bottom halves, followed by a couple of lettuce leaves and the upper roll halves. Yields 4 servings.

PEELING SWEET RED BELL PEPPER

Cut a slit in the pepper to allow steam to escape. Place pepper on a cookie sheet and broil, turning as the surface blisters and darkens, or skewer and roast over a stove burner. Seal the roasted pepper in a plastic bag and chill in the freezer for 10 minutes to steam its skin loose. Remove from freezer and peel.

MESQUITE-GRILLED CHICKEN SANDWICH WITH GRUYERE & SUN-DRIED TOMATOES

3 chicken breast halves, boned and skinned

4 ounces of Black Forest Ham (available at fine German delicatessens), julienne-cut.

1-1/2 cups grated Gruyère cheese

1 sweet red bell pepper, roasted, peeled (directions follow) and diced

1/2 cup sun-dried tomatoes (reserve oil for dressing), diced

1 to 2 tablespoons capers

Vinaigrette (recipe follows)

Pesto Mayonnaise (recipe follows)

4 French rolls, split and toasted

Romaine lettuce leaves

VINAIGRETTE

2 tablespoons fresh lemon juice
1/2 teaspoon salt
1/2 teaspoon Dijon mustard
Freshly ground black pepper
Worcestershire sauce
1/2 cup olive oil, preferably from a jar
  of sun-dried tomatoes

PESTO MAYONNAISE

1 cup packed basil leaves
2 cloves garlic
1 tablespoon chopped parsley
2 tablespoons pine nuts
2 tablespoons grated Parmesan cheese
1/4 teaspoon salt
1/4 cup olive oil
1/2 cup mayonnaise

MESQUITE-GRILLED PORK WITH
  SPINACH PRESTO SAUCE

4 large boneless loin pork chops (about
  1-1/2 pounds total)
Oil
1 long French baguette, cut into 4 pieces
Salt and pepper to taste
1/2 cup Spinach Presto Sauce (page 167)
1 cup each: finely shredded carrot, turnip
4 romaine lettuce leaves

In a small bowl, combine lemon juice, salt, mustard, pepper (to taste) and several dashes of Worcestershire sauce. Blend well with wire whip. Continue whipping as you add olive oil. Adjust seasonings. Yields about 2/3 cup.

Vinaigrette can be made up to 2 or 3 days ahead, covered, and stored in the refrigerator.

Combine basil, garlic and parsley in a blender jar; chop fine. Add pine nuts, Parmesan and salt; blend. With machine running, slowly pour in olive oil and continue blending until a smooth paste is formed. Yields about 1-1/2 cups pesto.

The Pesto Mayonaise is composed of 4 parts mayonnaise to 1 part pesto. For 4 servings, combine 1/2 cup fine-quality mayonnaise with 2 tablespoons pesto.

Mesquite-Grilled Pork with Spinach Presto Sauce

Place each chop between 2 sheets of waxed paper and pound to 1/4-inch thickness. Brush chops with oil, then grill quickly over mesquite coals, turning once, until done. Salt and pepper to taste.

Slice each of the baguette pieces lengthwise, and toast over the coals. Spread both halves of each section with some of the Spinach Presto Sauce. Arrange a chop on each bottom half, trimming the chop to fit the bread. Top each sandwich with the shredded carrot and turnip, a lettuce leaf, and the upper portion of bread. Yields 4 servings.

Sausage & Leek Sauté

This makes a wonderful, quick, late evening supper —delicious after a strenuous day of outdoor play.

Sauté sausage rounds and leeks in salad oil over medium to medium-high heat until sausages are golden and leeks are tender, about 7 minutes. Reduce heat and add the wine kraut, cooking until it is heated through.

To assemble, spread each bun with mustard and mayonnaise. Place one fourth of the sausage mixture on the lower half of each bun, top with a portion of the cheese, some shredded lettuce, and the upper portion of the bun. Yields 4 servings.

SAUSAGE & LEEK SAUTE

1 pound smoked sausage (beef, pork, turkey or chicken), cut into 1/4-inch slices

2 cups sliced fresh leeks

1 tablespoon salad oil

1 cup rinsed and drained wine kraut (or good-quality sauerkraut)

Mustard

Mayonnaise

4 split and toasted Kaiser buns

1-1/2 cups shredded Swiss cheese

Shredded lettuce

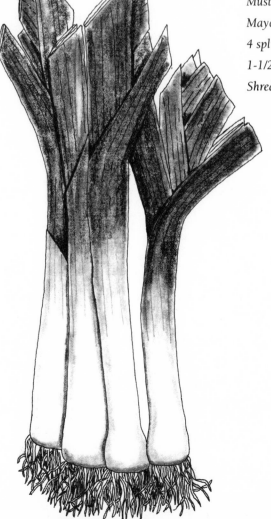

Egg Scramble with Red Peppers

EGG SCRAMBLE WITH RED PEPPERS

2 slices bacon

1/4 cup chopped red sweet bell pepper

*2 tablespoons finely minced shallots or
    green onion*

2 eggs

2 tablespoons milk

Dash salt

About 1/3 cup shredded Cheddar cheese

Split and toasted French roll

Mayonnaise and ketchup

*Lettuce and tomato slices for garnish
    (optional)*

Cook bacon in a small skillet over medium-high heat until crisp. Remove to paper towels to drain well. Remove all but 1 tablespoon of bacon drippings from pan. Add pepper and onion and sauté until soft, 4 to 5 minutes.

Meanwhile, combine eggs, milk and dash of salt in a small bowl; whip gently until eggs are beaten. Pour eggs into the pan with the peppers and onion and cook gently, pulling edges inward and tipping the pan so that the uncooked portion of egg moves to the outside. When enough of the egg mixture has solidified, turn with a spatula to lightly cook the upper side. In this manner, the eggs will have a consistency somewhere between an omelette and scrambled. Right before lifting the eggs from the pan, sprinkle the cheese down the center of the mixture and fold some of the egg over on top so that the heat of the cooked eggs will partially melt the cheese.

To assemble sandwich, first spread both halves of the roll with mayonnaise and ketchup. Layer the egg mixture and bacon strips on the bottom half. Garnish with lettuce and tomatoes, if desired, before adding the upper portion of the roll. Yields 1 serving.

"The Chiles" Burger Grande— A Variation on a Theme

Several years ago I was developing recipes for an article on chiles. Setting out to cross the richness of a cheesy chile relleno with the zestiness of a hot pickled pepper, I came up with a humdinger of a hybrid. Imagine, if you will, roasted and peeled Anaheim chiles, marinated for several hours in a cumin and garlic vinaigrette, then stuffed with a velvety mixture of cream cheese, green onion and Monterey Jack cheese. Now top each plump package with a generous dollop of salsa and shredded cheese, and before serving, pass them under the broiler until the cheeses melt together.

To say they were a hit would be an understatement. In fact, early on the family stopped referring to the dish by its given name, Stuffed Anaheim Chiles with Cream Cheese Filling, which couldn't stand the traffic. Now it is simply THE CHILES.

When I demonstrated the preparation of THE CHILES on a Portland, Oregon television show, the studio audience seemed equally captivated. During a commercial break, a soft-spoken lady gingerly raised her hand and asked the floor director whether the audience would be able to sample the recipe. "Why, uh, no," said this professional media person, mumbling on about liability insurance and county health department policy. However, regulations seemed less prominent in the director's mind after the show, as she rushed the set, paper plate in hand. Even the petite co-host managed to fork down several mouthsful before her next segment.

Later, when my young niece came to town for a visit, I asked her what she had at the top of her agenda.

"Learning how to make THE CHILES," she said. Besides being a genuine fan of the dish, Meredith was visualizing the leverage that would flow from being the only one in her family of six to know how to produce it. "It'll drive Bryan crazy," she smiled, visualizing the riches she could extort from her older brother. "Just a bite,

Merrrr! Please!" How charming. We got right to work.

Since then I've worked on variations. The following sandwich spin-off is the result of those efforts. However, I feel it's necessary to add that my husband, who is usually pretty helpful in such matters, was no help at all. When I asked him how he thought THE CHILES could be improved, he merely replied, "More."

"THE CHILES" BURGER GRANDE—
A VARIATION ON A THEME

2 pounds lean ground beef
8 French rolls, split and toasted
Condiments: Mustard, mayonnaise,
  ketchup, tomatoes, shredded lettuce,
  sliced onions
THE CHILES (recipe follows)

Shape the meat into 8 thin, rectangular patties (the same shape as the French rolls, only larger to allow for shrinkage during cooking). Grill or fry the patties until cooked to desired doneness. At the same time, finish THE CHILES by broiling them, as described in the recipe, and slicing off their stem ends.

Meanwhile, have diners dress their rolls with their preferred condiments. To assemble the burgers, place a cooked pattie on each prepared roll, then top with one of the broiled CHILES and the other half of the roll. Yields 8 servings.

THE CHILES

8 Anaheim chiles, each one measuring
  5 or 6 inches long
2 cups red or white wine vinegar
1/2 cup salad oil
1 tablespoon whole cumin seeds
2 cloves garlic, peeled and lightly
  crushed
2 teaspoons sugar
1 teaspoon salt
Cream Cheese filling (recipe follows)
Salsa (commercial brand or homemade)
1 cup shredded Monterey Jack cheese

Cut one lengthwise slit in each chile (to prevent bursting), then roast either under the heating element in the oven, or over a stove burner, turning as each side blisters. Place the roasted chiles in a plastic bag and store in a freezer for 10 minutes so steam can loosen the skins; remove from freezer. Gently slip off skins, cut each chile open lengthwise (leave an inch uncut at each end) and remove seeds. DO NOT CUT OFF THE STEM END! Lay the chiles out in a single layer in a plastic container with a flat bottom.

In a saucepan, combine vinegar, salad oil, cumin seeds, garlic cloves, sugar and salt; bring to boil and simmer 10 minutes; remove from heat and allow to cool about 5 minutes. Pour the marinade through a strainer over the chiles, cover well and refrigerate at least 8 hours. Chiles can be refrigerated for up to one week before use.

When ready to serve, place the drained chiles in a baking pan. Stuff each chile with one eighth of the cream cheese filling, spoon on a couple tablespoons of salsa, then sprinkle with 1/4 cup of the Monterey Jack cheese. Broil until cheese is lightly golden; serve.

Delicious as a first course or side dish for an elegant American Southwest or Mexican meal. Also makes a nice light meal when served with a salad. Yields 8 servings.

Cream together 1 (8 ounce) package softened cream cheese and 1 raw egg yolk. Stir in 2 or 3 chopped green onions (about 1/2 cup) and 1/2 cup shredded Monterey Jack cheese.

CREAM CHEESE FILLING

MENUS

A SCINTILLATING SUPPER FOR FRIENDS

Asparagus with Sautéed Mushrooms (page 136)

Harvest Thyme Beef Sandwiches (page 112)
Broiled Tomato Halves with Parmesan
Caesar Salad (page 156)

Chocolate Mousse

SIMPLY ENTERTAINING

Cheese Bread with Spinach Presto Sauce (page 135)

Mesquite-Grilled Chicken Salad with Teriyaki Onions (page 114)
Sliced Garden-Fresh Tomatoes
With Sesame & Poppy Seed Vinaigrette (page 170)

Hazelnut Wafers (page 174)

A CASUAL DINNER ON THE DECK

Fresh-fried Tortilla Chips and Veggies
With Salsa and Guacamole (page 169)
Frozen Margaritas or Sparkling Sodas

Leek & Shrimp Supper On a Roll (page 113)
Spinach Salad With 5-minute Egg (page 155)

Fresh Fruit Tarts

A SUNSET SUPPER

Farmer Style Cheese Soup (page 154)

Grilled Pork with Spinach Presto Sauce (page 167)
Tossed Green Salad

Fresh Fruit Bowl of Kiwi and Oranges
In Almond Liqueur

Chapter 8

Little Nibbles

Depending on ingredients and the occasion, nibble-sized sandwiches can fall anywhere between Casual and Uptown. Sometimes it's just a matter of presentation. After all, an onion sandwich doesn't strike you as particularly snazzy, now does it? Yet, James Beard took New York City by storm with an onion cocktail sandwich when he broke into the Big Apple in 1937. His "Onion Rings" were constructed from little rounds of thinly sliced brioche. Inside, nothing more than a film of fine mayonnaise and a paper-thin slice of onion, lightly salted. Outside, a frilly green wreath created by first dipping the edges in mayonnaise, then rolling them through minced parsley. The combination of understatement and flair bowled over sophisticated Manhattanites.

Grandma Skinner's Scones

As you may know, scones are Britain's contribution to the biscuit genre—and one of the best devices known for transporting strawberry jam from jar to mouth. For me, however, the making of scones is a comfort-ritual. As I stand by the griddle watching my tender delectables brown and plump, I feel enfolded in the arms of family.

Invariably, the time I mailed a package of freshly baked scones home for my mother's birthday comes to mind. You might think that an odd gift, but I had no doubt it would rank right up there with the red and white polka-dot cardboard wallet I stapled together for her in third grade. Both were gifts from the heart; and if there is one thing at which all mothers excel, it's recognizing gifts from the heart. You see, when my mother's mother was alive, steaming scones hot off the griddle were a part of most Saturdays, either for breakfast or late afternoon tea.

Two of Grandma's sisters thought they knew how to make scones. After all, they, too, were born in Scotland. But everyone concurred that Grandma Skinner's were the best. She had the touch. I know, because I used to stand there—eyeballs at bowl level—watching her lightly mix the buttermilk into the flour with a knife. Only a knife would do, she'd explain, because forks and spoons worked the dough too thoroughly, making the scones heavy and dry.

She'd gently lift the lumpy dough from the bowl and lay the slightly sticky mass on a flour-dusted board. Working quickly, she'd quarter it, roll and pat each section into half-inch thick rounds, then cut each round into four triangles. By the time the sixteenth triangle was formed, the griddle would be hot enough to make water droplets dance frenetically across its surface.

As the scones came off the griddle, they'd be tucked into a soft tea towel to cool. But they rarely cooled long because a scone is at its peak only so long as butter can still melt upon its tender surface. We'd quickly slice them, slather on butter and strawberry jam, and sandwich the halves back together, swirls of butter and jam oozing out the sides.

Unfortunately, the experience is never again to be duplicated in our family because, like I said, only Grandma Skinner had the touch. Of all the poor seconds, mine are considered the best—probably because I so often watched the master herself at work. But Grandma's were perfect.

So you see, there was more wrapped up inside that Express Mail package than a bunch of biscuits. The next day I got a call. Over the long-distance static came my mother's voice. "Good morning," she began cheerily. There was a long pause, and then a muffled, "Guess what I'm doing?"

I only wish I could have been there to pass the jam.

GRANDMA SKINNER'S SCONES

3 cups flour

1-1/2 teaspoons salt

1-1/2 teaspoons baking soda

1-1/2 teaspoons cream of tartar

1 teaspoon sugar

1 tablespoon butter

1-1/2 cups buttermilk

Sift all of the dry ingredients together into a bowl. By hand, rub the butter into the flour, making small cornmeal-like granules. Add buttermilk all at once. Working quickly but gently, mix with a dinner knife (spoons overwork the dough, making a tough scone) until the dough is just barely mixed. Add a little more buttermilk if necessary, but don't make the dough sticky.

Divide the dough into quarters. On a floured board, roll out each quarter into a circle 1/4-inch thick. Cut each circle into quarters. Bake the scones in batches on a medium-hot (350°) lightly greased griddle for a few minutes, until lightly golden. Turn and cook the other side. Now brown all of the edges in turn by standing the triangles up and leaning them against each other for about 30 seconds. As the scones come off the griddle, cool in a tea towel until ready to use. Yields 16 scones.

Scottish scones are delicious straight off the griddle with butter and fresh strawberry jam or lemon curd.

Asparagus Nibbles

These wonderful little make-ahead hors d'oeuvres are a treat to assemble in the spring when asparagus hits the market. You can store them in your freezer for a time later in the year when the taste would really hit the spot.

ASPARAGUS NIBBLES

25 fresh asparagus spears

Salt to taste

25 slices white, whole wheat, or Oregon Bleu (page 165) bread

8 ounces cream cheese, softened

3 ounces Oregon Bleu cheese, softened

1 egg

1 to 1-1/2 cups butter, melted

Blanch asparagus spears (page 27, "BLANCH IT"), until barely tender, 3 to 5 minutes. Drain immediately and plunge into cold water to stop the cooking process.

Remove crusts from bread and flatten slices with a rolling pin.

In a medium bowl, combine cheeses and egg, blending with an electric beater. Spread mixture evenly over bread slices. Trim asparagus spears to same length as bread slices, and then place one spear on each slice and roll up, jelly roll fashion. Dip each roll in melted butter to coat all sides, and place on a cookie sheet. Freeze rolls until hard, then re-package in freezer-storage containers.

When ready to bake, cut frozen rolls into thirds and bake (while still frozen) in 400° oven for 15 minutes or until lightly browned. Serve immediately. Yields 75 pieces.

Basil & Green Peppercorn Cheese Spread

Place cheeses and heavy cream in blender or food processor and process until creamy. Transfer mixture to a bowl, then stir in the basil, peppercorns and garlic.

With a small biscuit cutter, cut 35 of the pumpernickel slices into 1-1/4 to 1-1/2 inch diameter rounds. You should get 2 rounds from each slice, for a total of 70.

Arrange half the rounds on a board and spread each one with about 1 tablespoon of the cheese spread, then top with a second round and press gently.

Set out a plate of mayonnaise and a plate of chopped chives. Roll half the circumference of each sandwich through mayonnaise, and then through chives. Chill until ready to serve. Yields about 2 cups of spread, enough for about 35 sandwiches.

BASIL & GREEN PEPPERCORN CHEESE SPREAD

8 ounces feta cheese

8 ounces cream cheese, softened

1 tablespoon heavy cream

2 tablespoons fresh basil, minced

2 tablespoons coarsely chopped green peppercorns (they come packed in water and can be purchased in the specialty-food sections of most supermarkets)

1 clove garlic, finely minced

1 loaf thinly sliced pumpernickel bread

Mayonnaise

1/2 cup snipped chives

Little Bitty Burgers

These little bitty burgers are perfect for casual entertaining on the deck or patio. Grill up a platter-full of little patties, then set them out with a variety of condiments and fresh little buns. Most bakeries—even those located inside major supermarkets—will make hamburger buns sized to your specifications as long as you give them at least 24 hours notice.

One pound of lean ground beef will yield eight 2-3/4 inch uncooked patties. There will be some shrinkage during cooking, but arrange for the baker to make your buns closer to the 2-3/4 inch size (or slightly larger) so diners will have room to build their little bitty burgers into something spectacular with condiments.

What kinds of condiments? The usual pickles, tomatoes, onions, mustard, ketchup and mayonnaise, of course. But baby greens (growers call it mesclun), avocado slices, sliced olives, shredded cheese, freshly-cooked diced bacon, rings of red, yellow, and green sweet bell peppers, sliced mushrooms and sprouts are also excellent touches.

As an hors d'oeuvre, figure on 2 burgers per person.

Other Little Bitty Bun Ideas

Once you've found a baker willing to make little bitty hamburger buns (3 inches or smaller), then you've opened up a whole new area for nibble cuisine. Just about any chicken salad you like on a big piece of bread will be wonderful on a bitty bun. So will egg salad and tuna salad. By using a 2- or 3-inch round cookie/biscuit cutter, you can cut luncheon meats and cheeses to the appropriate size.

Here are a few simple fillings for bitty buns:

CORNED BEEF

Combine 2 cups finely chopped freshly cooked corned beef, 1 cup chopped celery, 1/2 cup mayonnaise, 1/4 cup chopped green onion, 3 tablespoons hot dog relish, and 1 tablespoon stone-ground mustard. Adjust seasonings and consistency by adding more mayonnaise, mustard or relish to taste. Yields about 2-3/4 cups filling.

ROAST BEEF

Combine 2 cups diced deli-cut roast beef, 1/2 cup mayonnaise, 1/4 cup minced onion, and 2 tablespoons prepared horseradish. Assemble the bitty sandwiches by spreading a portion of the filling on bottom of each bun, then top with a thin tomato slice and a small piece of lettuce. Spread upper bun with a small amount of mayonnaise and horseradish. Yields about 3 cups filling.

Prepare Egg Salad Louie! Louie! (page 155). Stir in 1/2 cup fresh Oregon shrimp or fresh Oregon Dungeness crab, and 1/4 cup finely chopped dill pickle. Yields about 2-1/2 cups filling.

HIGH SEAS EGG SALAD LOUIE! LOUIE!

Hanky Pankies

This recipe is from a friend's mother-in-law. It's ages old.

In a skillet, sauté the hamburger and sausage until browned; drain well, then add the cheese cubes, oregano, garlic, salt and onion salt to taste. Heat through until cheese melts. Spread on rye bread, sprinkle with Parmesan cheese and broil until golden. Yields about 50 Hanky Pankies.

These freeze fantastically. After spreading the mixture on rye, seal in airtight containers and freeze. When ready to use, place on baking sheet, sprinkle with Parmesan, and broil.

HANKY PANKIES

2 pounds hamburger

1 pound ground sausage

1 pound cubed Velveeta cheese

2 loaves cocktail rye bread

Oregano

Garlic

Onion salt

Salt

Grated Parmesan cheese

Mini Meatloaf Sandwiches

MINI MEATLOAF SANDWICHES

1 meatloaf (page 147), thoroughly
*   chilled*

2 loaves cocktail French bread, sliced

About 1 cup mayonnaise

About 1/2 cup mustard (Dijon, stone-
*   ground, or prepared)*

5 tomatoes, thinly sliced

2 onions, finely minced

1 head romaine lettuce, broken into
*   appropriate-sized leaves*

Cut meatloaf into 16 slices. Halve each slice to fit cocktail-sized bread.

Spread each bread slice with mayonnaise and mustard. Top half the bread with slices of the meatloaf and tomato. Sprinkle on the onion, add small leaves of lettuce, and finish each sandwich with a second slice of bread. Yields 32 sandwiches.

Mini Oregon Bleu Clubs

MINI OREGON BLEU CLUBS

16 slices pumpernickel bread

8 slices white bread

1/3 cup butter, softened

8 thin slices quality ham

8 thin slices Gruyère cheese, or other
*   quality Swiss cheese*

Dijon-style mustard

Mayonnaise

3 tomatoes, thinly sliced

3 ounces Oregon Bleu cheese, softened

16 cocktail onions

Using a 3-inch round cutter, cut 2 rounds from each slice of pumpernickel and white bread. Butter the pumpernickel rounds on one side only, and the white bread rounds on both sides. Now, using the same cutter, cut 16 rounds from the ham and 16 rounds from the Gruyère cheese.

To assemble sandwiches, layer 1 ham round on each of the 16 slices of buttered pumpernickel. Top with a Gruyère round, mustard, and mayonnaise and another round of ham. Add one of the white bread rounds, another Gruyère round, a tomato slice, and a sprinkling of bleu cheese. Finish with a pumpernickel round, then secure each sandwich with a wooden pick on which a cocktail onion has been skewered. Yields 16 mini clubs.

Chicken Liver Pâtè Sandwich

Sauté onion in butter over medium heat until transparent. Add livers and cook until slightly browned, then mash with fork. Place mixture in a blender with the egg yolks and cream and remaining ingredients. Purée until smooth.

Pour purée into a well-greased 9- by 5-inch baking pan. Cover top with buttered waxed paper and place in a pan of water. Bake in 300° oven for 1-1/2 hours. Remove from oven and cool for 20 minutes. Then cover tightly and refrigerate 24 to 48 hours before serving.

To assemble, cut the pâté into 1/2-inch thick slices, then quarter each slice. Place a slice of pâté on each piece of baguette, pressing down slightly to spread the mixture over the surface of the bread. Top with a dollop of mustard and a slice of pickle. Yields 64 servings.

CHICKEN LIVER PATE
SANDWICH

1 cup finely chopped onion

3 tablespoons butter

*1 pound chicken livers, drained, with
    membranes removed*

2 egg yolks

1/4 cup heavy cream

2 tablespoons flour

2 teaspoons Worcestershire sauce

1 teaspoon dried tarragon

1 teaspoon salt

1/2 teaspoon white pepper

1/3 cup dry sherry

*2 baguettes French bread, cut into 64
    1/4-inch thick slices*

*8 baby dill pickles, cut diagonally into
    64 1/4-inch thick slices*

About 1/3 cup Dijon mustard

Oriental Chicken Pockets

ORIENTAL CHICKEN POCKETS

2 pounds boned chicken thigh meat

2 tablespoons butter

2 tablespoons soy sauce

1/2 cup mayonnaise, more as needed

1 teaspoon Chinese mustard

1 cup chopped celery

1/3 cup chopped green onion

2 teaspoons chile and garlic paste

1 tablespoon toasted sesame seeds

2 cups alfalfa sprouts

24 mini-pocket breads

Dice raw chicken into 1/2-inch cubes. Place in a baking pan with the butter and soy sauce and bake in 375° oven for about 30 minutes. Stir the chunks of chicken once or twice after the butter has melted to evenly distribute the juices, and then baste the surface occasionally during cooking.

Let chicken mixture cool, then coarsely chop into slightly smaller pieces (not smaller than 1/4-inch). Combine the chicken with the mayonnaise, mustard, celery, onion, chile paste, and sesame seeds. Up to 4 hours before serving, stuff mini-pockets with alfalfa sprouts and about 1 heaping tablespoon of the filling. To keep pocket bread from getting soggy if making more than an hour ahead, place the filled sandwiches on a tray with the alfalfa sprout side down, so the filling won't be resting too firmly against the bread. Cover and refrigerate until ready to serve. Yields 24 pockets.

Salmon Spread on Brioche

I originally developed my Salmon Spread as a quick and simple way to use up a large amount of leftover barbecued salmon. It's worth making, even if you have to cook up a fresh batch of salmon.

SALMON SPREAD ON BRIOCHE

3 cups fresh cooked salmon

1-1/2 tablespoons lemon juice

8 ounces cream cheese . . .

Place the salmon, lemon juice, cream cheese, onion, liquid smoke, and salt in a blender or food processor and blend until smooth. Pack into a bowl and refrigerate at least 1 hour. May be prepared up to 24 hours ahead.

To assemble sandwiches, slice the brioche loaf into 45

1/4-inch slices. Then, with a small cutter, cut the slices into rounds (about 1-1/4 to 1-1/2 inches in diameter). You should get 2 rounds from each slice, for a total of 90. Arrange the rounds on a board and spread them with the mayonnaise, followed by a sprinkling of dill. On half of them, spread about 1 tablespoon of the Salmon Spread, then top with a second round of brioche and press gently.

Set out a plate of mayonnaise and a plate of chopped chives. Roll half the circumference of each sandwich through mayonnaise, and then through chives. Chill until ready to serve. Yields about 3-1/2 cups spread, enough for about 45 sandwiches.

1 tablespoon finely minced chopped onion

1/8 teaspoon liquid smoke

1/2 teaspoon salt (more to taste)

1 brioche loaf (or substitute any compact light-flavored bread, such as challah, a Jewish egg bread), chilled

Mayonnaise

Dill

1/2 cup chopped chives

Cheese Bread with Spinach Presto Sauce

Spread the surface of each baguette half with a layer of the Spinach Presto Sauce. Place the bread halves on a baking sheet; sprinkle with cheese, and bake in 375° oven for 10 to 20 minutes, until hot, bubbly and very golden in color. Cut into slices (for dinner) or 1-inch chunks (for hors d'oeuvres) and serve.

CHEESE BREAD WITH SPINACH PRESTO SAUCE

1 or 2 French baguettes, sliced lengthwise

1/2 cup Spinach Presto Sauce (page 167)

1 heaping cup shredded sharp Cheddar cheese

After spreading the Spinach Presto Sauce on the bread, sprinkle with chopped sun-dried tomatoes (the oil-pack variety), then sprinkle with cheese and bake as previously described.

SUN-DRIED TOMATO VARIATION

Asparagus with Sautéed Mushrooms

ASPARAGUS WITH SAUTEED
MUSHROOMS

3/4 pound fresh mushrooms, sliced

2 tablespoons butter

2 tablespoons olive oil

1 large clove garlic, minced

1/4 cup dry white wine (or 2 tablespoons brandy)

1 tablespoon Worcestershire sauce

1/4 teaspoon salt

1/4 teaspoon hot pepper sauce

1/4 teaspoon white pepper

1 pound asparagus, cooked just until
   tender (page 27), plunged into cold
   water to cool, and drained

1 baguette, sliced into 1/4-inch thick
   rounds

In a large frying pan, sauté the mushrooms in the butter and olive oil over medium to medium-high heat until the mushrooms release their liquids and the liquid reduces, about 7 minutes. Reduce heat to medium, add garlic and sauté another minute. Add the wine, Worcestershire sauce, salt, hot pepper sauce, and white pepper; continue cooking until the sauce reduces and the mushrooms become very dark and richly flavored, at least 15 minutes. It's important to give the mushrooms this long cooking time to develop the flavor, so don't compromise.

Meanwhile, cut the asparagus spears diagonally into 1/2-inch thick pieces. After the mushrooms are done, gently add the asparagus and continue cooking just until the asparagus is heated through. Spoon the mushroom mixture onto a heated platter, surround with the baguette slices and serve immediately. Yields 6 to 8 servings as an appetizer.

NOTE: Once asparagus season is over, the sautéed mushrooms are still wonderful all by themselves with the baguette slices.

Surimi & Cream Cheese Snacks

Surimi by any other name—Krab, imitation crab, Krabb—is still fish processed to have the flavor and texture of crab. But in the right recipe, it can be a very good product, at a fourth the cost of the genuine article.

Melt cream cheese over medium-low heat. Stir in mayonnaise, surimi, sherry, onion, mustard and Worcestershire sauce.

Arrange bread slices on a cookie sheet and broil until golden. Spread each slice with 2 tablespoons of the surimi mixture. Broil until golden and bubbly. Yields 24 snacks.

The surimi mixture can be prepared up to 24 hours in advance and stored covered in a refrigerator. Before spreading it onto bread, you may want to soften it slightly by gently reheating it on the stove or in a microwave oven.

SURIMI & CREAM CHEESE SNACKS

8 ounces cream cheese

1/2 cup mayonnaise

1/2 pound surimi, rinsed and drained

1 tablespoon sherry

1 tablespoon finely minced onion

1 teaspoon Dijon mustard

1/2 teaspoon Worcestershire sauce

1 baguette, sliced into 1/4-inch thick rounds (or 1 loaf cocktail French bread)

Chapter 9

*R*estaurant Specialties

W hen I requested sandwich recipes from these restaurants, I had their creative spirits in mind, rather than their menus. They represent only a small sampling of Oregon eateries, but what a group! From Timberline Lodge, the popular resort on Mt. Hood's southern slope, to Portland's American Southwest hot spot, Casa-U-Betcha, to the Greenleaf Deli in Ashland, with its throngs of Shakespeare aficionados, variety is the name of the game.

Casa-U-Betcha

Portland

John Huyck, Chef

Roast Vegetable & Wild Mushroom Quesadilla

ROAST VEGETABLE & WILD
MUSHROOM QUESADILLA

1 medium-sized eggplant, peeled and
cut lengthwise into 1/4-inch slices

4 Roma tomatoes, cored and quartered
lengthwise

1 red onion, peeled and cut into quarters

6 ounces wild mushrooms, preferably
chanterelles

1 red sweet bell pepper

2 poblano chiles

1 bunch basil (about 1/2 cup) finely
chopped

Zest of 3 lemons

Salt

Pepper

4 cups shredded Monterey Jack cheese
(1 pound)

Red Chile Sauce (recipe follows)

2 tablespoons olive oil

1 cup sour cream

8 (8-inch) flour tortillas

Lightly salt the eggplant and place in a colander to drain for 20 minutes. Then, under the oven broiler or on an open grill, cook the slices for about 2 minutes, watching carefully so they don't burn. If neither broiler nor grill is available, sauté lightly in olive oil. After cooking, set aside to cool.

Place the tomatoes and onions in separate pans and roast in a 450° oven, 20 minutes for the tomatoes and 30 minutes for the onions; set aside to cool.

Briefly sauté the mushrooms in olive oil; set aside to cool.

Over an open flame or under the oven broiler, roast the bell pepper and the chiles evenly on all sides until the skin gets black, then put in a bowl and cover for 20 minutes to steam skins from flesh. Remove peppers from bowl and gently peel away the skin; remove seeds and set aside.

Dice all of the vegetables into 1/2-inch squares and place in mixing bowl. Add basil and lemon zest, mixing well, then season with salt and pepper to taste.

For each quesadilla: Place 1/3 cup of the vegetable mixture in a large sauté pan and heat through; add about 1/4 cup of the Red Chile Sauce and stir. Place an 8-inch flour tortilla in a pan, over medium-high heat. Add 1/2 cup of the shredded cheese in the center of the tortilla, and spread it out to within 1/2 inch of the edge. When the cheese starts to melt pour the vegetable mixture in the center and fold the tortilla in half. Remove the quesadilla to serving plate, then drizzle with sour cream for garnish. Yields 8 servings.

This dish can also be done on the outdoor grill and makes a wonderful accompaniment to barbecues.

Roast chiles in a 350° oven for 3 minutes, being careful not to burn them. Remove stems, scrape out the seeds and place in pot with the 2 quarts of water; boil for 20 minutes.

In a separate pan, sauté the garlic cloves, onions and carrots in the olive oil until onions are translucent. Meanwhile, when the chiles are through boiling, strain from the water and place in the pan with the other vegetables, oregano, and tomato paste. Add enough fresh warm water to cover, and continue simmering until all of the vegetables are very tender; remove mixture from burner and cool slightly. In blender or food processor, purée the mixture, then strain through a sieve into a bowl and season to taste with the salt, pepper and sugar.

If more heat is desired, add 2 or 3 Japanese chiles to the sauce when you first begin cooking it.

RED CHILE SAUCE

4 ounces ancho chile pods (dried Poblano chiles from specialty food section or market)

4 ounces New Mexican chile pods (from specialty food section or market)

2 quarts water

6 cloves peeled garlic

1/2 white onion, peeled and diced

1/2 carrot, peeled and diced

5 tablespoons olive oil

1 tablespoon Mexican oregano

1/2 cup tomato paste

Salt

Black pepper

Sugar

The Heathman Restaurant
Portland
George Tate, Executive Chef

Heathman's Rosemary Chicken Salad Sandwich

HEATHMAN'S ROSEMARY CHICKEN
SALAD SANDWICH

4 poached chicken breasts, cooled and
*   chopped (recipe follows)*
1 tablespoon chopped fresh rosemary
1 tart green apple, cored and finely
*   chopped*
1 cup mayonnaise (recipe follows)
1 stalk celery, finely chopped
Salt, pepper and fresh lemon juice to
*   taste*
1 green onion, finely chopped
8 slices whole wheat bread
Garnishes: tomato slices, water cress or
*   lettuce leaves*

POACHED CHICKEN

4 boned and skinned chicken breasts,
*   with all fat and membranes*
*   removed*
1/2 white onion
1 stalk celery, coarsely chopped
1/2 bay leaf
1/2 teaspoon black peppercorns
2 sprigs fresh rosemary

Combine all ingredients except garnishes, using only half the mayonnaise. Season with salt, lemon juice and pepper as desired. Add remaining mayonnaise to adjust to desired consistency.

To serve, place chicken salad on 4 slices of bread with sliced tomato, water cress or lettuce. Top with remaining bread. Yields 4 servings. Serve with chilled fresh fruit.

Place chicken breasts in a pot with just enough water to cover them. Add remaining ingredients. Cover and poach just until chicken is firm but tender, about 20 minutes. Reserve a little of the liquid for use in the mayonnaise.

Place egg yolks and whole egg in food processor. With motor running, slowly add the mixed oils. Lighten the mayonnaise by adding about 1/2 teaspoon of the chicken poaching liquid. Season with fresh lemon juice, salt and Tabasco.

MAYONNAISE

2 egg yolks

1 whole egg

1/2 cup each light olive oil and salad oil, mixed

About 1/2 teaspoon of reserved chicken poaching liquid

Fresh lemon juice, salt, and Tabasco to taste

Connie's Restaurant & Catering
Philomath
Connie Jager, Owner/Chef

Italian Teaser

Split the roll. Brush top half with the Italian dressing. On lower half, layer salami, ham, rings of bell pepper and onion, and end with provolone. Replace top half and heat the sandwich in a microwave oven, or in a 400° conventional oven, just until cheese begins to melt. Remove from oven, take off top and spread with mayonnaise. Then add the additional garnishes, replace top and serve. Yields 1 serving.

ITALIAN TEASER

1 Italian roll, if available, otherwise substitute French roll

Italian dressing

Several slices each: salami, ham, green sweet bell peppers, onion and provolone cheese

Mayonnaise

Additional garnishes: leaf lettuce, tomato slices, pickled Greek pepperoncini

The Greenleaf Restaurant
Ashland
Chef Freducinni (A.K.A. Fred Morgan)

The Greenleaf Pollo Piccata Sandwich

THE GREENLEAF POLLO PICCATA
SANDWICH

1/4 pound boneless, skinless chicken
breast, pounded to even thickness and
sliced into 1/2-inch wide strips
1/2 cup seasoned bread crumbs, finely
ground (recipe below)
1 tablespoon sweet butter
1 tablespoon olive oil
1/2 teaspoon capers
Squeeze of lemon
1/4 teaspoon fresh chopped garlic
Chopped parsley
1 fresh French roll, split
Mayonnaise
Garnishes: sliced tomato, crisp romaine
lettuce leaf

SEASONED BREAD CRUMBS

In medium-hot sauté pan, melt the butter with the olive oil. Add garlic and sauté for a moment. Dredge the chicken strips through the bread crumb mixture and sauté, turning once after about 30 to 45 seconds, when lightly browned. Finish by adding capers and squeeze of lemon. The chicken will cook quickly, depending on its thickness; don't overcook.

Spread the roll halves with mayonnaise. Place the chicken on the bread and dress with the juices and capers from the pan. Add the suggested garnishes, then sprinkle with a little chopped parsley and serve open faced. Yields one serving.

Mix together 1-1/2 tablespoons finely grated Parmesan cheese, 5-1/2 tablespoons fine sourdough crumbs, and 1 tablespoon chopped parsley.

Valley Restaurant

Corvallis

Mary Bentley, Manager/Chef

Valley Melt—A Vegetarian Treat

In small skillet, sauté the mushrooms and onions in salad oil until softened and mushrooms are slightly golden; set aside.

Top one bread slice with the Thousand Island dressing. Top other slice with the cole slaw mixture. Divide the mushroom mixture between the two sides, then place a slice of cheese on each portion. Lightly brush a grill or frying pan with margarine, then place both portions on the grill (with the cheese side up). Cover the sandwiches with a large lid and cook until the cheese is melted and the bread is crisp. Carefully put the sandwich together and cut in half. Serve with extra napkins. Yields 1 serving.

Coarsely chop cabbage, green onions, carrots and apples. Toss together. Combine mayonnaise, honey, salt and pepper in a separate bowl. Coat tossed vegetables with this dressing. Refrigerate until ready to use.

VALLEY MELT—A VEGETARIAN TREAT

About 1/2 cup thinly sliced mushrooms

1/4 cup minced onions

1/2 tablespoon salad oil

2 slices Bavarian rye or pumpernickel

2 1-ounce slices of Swiss cheese

1 tablespoon Thousand Island dressing

2 tablespoons Valley Cole Slaw
   (recipe follows)

VALLEY COLE SLAW

1 small green cabbage

3 green onions

2 large carrots

3 medium Gravenstein apples (or other
   tart variety)

2 cups mayonnaise

1/4 cup honey

Salt and pepper to taste

Steamboat Inn

Steamboat

Sharon Van Loan, Chef/Co-owner

Patricia Lee, Chef/Manager

Oregon Bay Shrimp English Muffins

*OREGON BAY SHRIMP ENGLISH
　　MUFFINS*

4 English muffins, split and toasted

2 cups fresh bay (Pacific) shrimp

4 teaspoons minced fresh parsley

1 teaspoon minced fresh cilantro

Dash salt and pepper

*1 ripe avocado, peeled, seeded and
　thinly sliced*

Dash hot pepper sauce

*1 cup shredded Tillamook Cheddar
　cheese*

Toss the bay shrimp with the cilantro, 2 teaspoons of the minced parsley and a dash of salt and pepper.

Lay the split and toasted English muffins on a baking sheet, face up. Divide the sliced avocado among the muffin halves and sprinkle with a dash of hot pepper sauce. Top each with 1/4 cup of the shrimp mixture and top with the grated cheese.

Place muffins in a 375° oven and bake just long enough to melt the cheese. Remove to serving platters and garnish with the remaining 2 teaspoons of minced parsley. Yields 4 servings.

This is a quick and easy lunch alternative that is particularly nice accompanied with a crisp green salad.

The Underground Gourmet Deli and Restaurant
Ashland
Mark Levin, Chef

Underground Deli Meatloaf Sandwich

In a bowl, combine bread crumbs, mustard, black pepper, garlic powder, basil and oregano. In a large bowl, combine eggs, ketchup, hot pepper sauce, Worcestershire sauce, Dijon mustard and horseradish. Mix in the onion and ground beef, then add the bread crumb mixture. Place mixture in 9- by 5-inch loaf pan and bake in 350° oven for 1 hour.

To assemble, lay 1/2-inch slice of meatloaf on bottom slice of bread, and top with cheese. If meat is cold, warm in microwave or conventional oven with the cheese on bottom half of sandwich. On top half, spread mayonnaise, mustard, a hint of horseradish, tomatoes, onions and lettuce. Close, cut in half, and serve with a dill pickle. Meatloaf yields 9 or 10 servings.

UNDERGROUND DELI MEATLOAF SANDWICH

1 cup fresh bread crumbs

1-1/2 teaspoons dry mustard

1 teaspoon black pepper

1-1/2 teaspoons garlic powder

1 tablespoon dried basil

1 tablespoon dried oregano

3 eggs

3/4 cup ketchup

1/2 teaspoon hot pepper sauce

1-1/2 teaspoons each: Worcestershire sauce, Dijon mustard, horseradish

1 cup chopped onion

2-1/2 pounds lean ground beef

Choice of sliced Jack, Swiss or Cheddar cheese

Choice of sourdough, whole wheat, rye, or white bread, or French roll

Mayonnaise

Garnishes: mustard, horseradish, tomato and onion slices, lettuce leaves

The Gallery Restaurant
Roseburg
Constance Frana, Chef/Owner

Layered Crêpe Torta

LAYERED CREPE TORTA

3 ounces chèvre

3 ounces cream cheese

About 16 crêpes (recipe follows)

2 ounces prosciutto ham, thinly sliced

1 bunch fresh basil (about 1 cup),
    washed and dried

1/3 cup sun dried tomatoes, drained and
    slivered

1/2 cup roasted red peppers

1/2 cup red onion, thinly sliced

1/3 cup Olivada, (or follow recipe for
    olive paste that follows)

12 fresh spinach leaves, washed and
    dried (tough stems removed)

1/4 cup pine nuts, finely chopped

CREPES

2 cups flour

2 cups milk

6 eggs

1/2 teaspoon salt

2 teaspoons finely chopped fresh
    rosemary

In a food processor, combine chèvre and cream cheese until smooth. Spread a small amount of cream cheese mixture on one side of a crêpe. Place crêpe on a flat plate or serving tray, cheese-side up. Layer half of the prosciutto on crêpe. Spread cream cheese mixture on a second crêpe. Lay the second crêpe, coated side down, on top of prosciutto. Spread cream cheese mixture on top of the second crêpe and layer with half of the basil. Continue building the stack by coating both sides of each crêpe with the cream cheese mixture while layering each crêpe with half of one of the remaining ingredients, except the pine nuts. Top final crêpe with remaining cream cheese mixture and sprinkle with finely chopped pine nuts. Cut into 6 wedges and serve with fresh fruit or a green salad.

Combine the flour, milk, eggs, and salt in a blender, and process until smooth. Add rosemary and stir. Transfer to another bowl and allow to sit for several hours or overnight in refrigerator.

Over medium heat, melt a small amount of butter in a 7-inch crêpe pan. When melted, wipe out excess with paper towel. Add scant 1/4 cup batter to pan and tilt to coat bottom of pan evenly. Cook until set and lightly browned on the bottom. Flip and briefly cook the other side. Set aside. Continue with the rest of the batter. Makes approximately 16 crêpes.

In food processor, combine 1/2 cup imported pitted ripe olives, 2 tablespoons extra–virgin olive oil and 2 cloves garlic. Purée until smooth.

OLIVE PASTE

Cajun Cafe & Bistro
Portland
Allen Levin, Owner

Muffuletta Sandwich with Olive Relish

Combine the olives, onion, garlic, oregano and parsley in a bowl. In a separate small bowl, blend the olive oil with the pickle juice, and then drizzle the mixture over the olive relish, adding additional oil and juice, if necessary, to completely immerse the relish. Marinate for several hours or days.

When ready to assemble sandwiches, slice the rolls lengthwise and spread both sides with drained relish. Layer on the meats and cheese, replace top and cut into fourths. Yields 4 servings.

MUFFULETTA SANDWICH WITH
  OLIVE RELISH

1 cup pitted Sicilian olives, roughly
  chopped
1 cup pimiento-stuffed olives, roughly
  chopped
1/2 cup chopped red onion
2 tablespoons minced fresh garlic
2 tablespoons chopped fresh oregano
2 tablespoons chopped fresh parsley
1-1/2 cups olive oil
1/4 cup pickle juice
2 soft 10-inch rolls
Salami, peppered ham, provolone cheese
  and prosciutto

Timberline Lodge

Government Camp

Leif Eric Benson, Executive Chef

Kraut Kunchen

KRAUT KUNCHEN

1 cup milk, heated to lukewarm

1/2 cup warm water (95-100° F)

1-1/2 teaspoons dry yeast

2 teaspoons sugar

4-5 cups flour

1 teaspoon salt

6 tablespoons softened butter

1-1/4 pounds ground beef

1/2 cup chopped onion

4 cups chopped green cabbage

Salt and black pepper to taste

Maggi seasoning to taste

About 2 teaspoons chicken base

Sweet hot mustard

Combine milk and hot water, and then add the yeast and sugar. Let mixture sit until it bubbles and foams, about 5 to 10 minutes.

Stir in 3 cups of the flour, the salt and the butter, then turn out onto a board and knead in enough of the remaining flour to achieve a smooth and elastic dough. This should take about 10 minutes. Place dough in lightly oiled bowl, turn once to coat, cover loosely with plastic, and allow to rise until doubled in volume, about 90 minutes. Meanwhile, brown the beef in large skillet. Part way through, remove drippings, add onion and continue to cook until onions are tender. Add cabbage and remaining seasonings, stirring to mix well; adjust seasonings to taste.

Divide dough into 6 portions and roll each portion into a 10-inch round. Place a heaping 1/2 cup of filling on one half of each round. Fold over and seal. Bake in 350° oven until golden brown, about 30 minutes. Serve with sweet, hot mustard.

Waddle's
Portland
Russ Waddle, Owner

The Waddler

Spread one side of each bread slice with Thousand Island dressing. On bottom slice, arrange the corned beef brisket. Add second slice of bread, with dressing side up. On the dressing side, arrange the sauerkraut and then the Swiss cheese. Top with third slice of bread, dressing side facing inward. Butter top slice with some softened butter.

Melt some additional butter in skillet and grill the sandwich on bottom side until golden. Gently flip and grill the buttered side until golden.

THE WADDLER

*3 slices Pierre's sour dough rye bread
   (or substitute a plain sourdough.)*
Thousand Island dressing
3 slices cooked corned beef brisket
*About 1/3 cup sauerkraut, drained,
   rinsed and heated*
Several slices Swiss cheese

Chapter 10

*B*asic Recipes

& Menu Accompaniments

Farmer Style Cheese Soup

FARMER STYLE CHEESE SOUP

1 tablespoon butter

1 cup thinly sliced celery

1/2 cup chopped green onions

2 tablespoons flour

3 cups milk

3 chicken bouillon cubes, crumbled

1/2 teaspoon paprika

1/2 teaspoon white pepper

3/4 teaspoon garlic salt

1/8 teaspoon nutmeg

1 cup grated Cheddar cheese

Melt butter in a skillet. Sauté celery and onion over medium heat until vegetables are tender-crisp, about 5 minutes. With wire whisk, stir in flour and cook for about 30 seconds, then whisk in milk and bouillon. Cook, stirring constantly, until mixture thickens and comes to a boil. Reduce heat and stir in paprika, pepper, garlic salt, nutmeg and cheese. Heat until cheese melts, but do not bring to a boil. Yields 1 quart soup, enough for 4 servings.

Source: The Oregon Dairy Council.

Waddle's Chicken à la Reine Soup

WADDLE'S CHICKEN à la REINE
   SOUP

4 cups water

1 cup chopped onion

1-1/2 cups chopped carrot

1 cup chopped celery

1/2 cup chopped green pepper

2 tablespoons chicken base

1/2 teaspoon white pepper

1 tablespoon sugar

3 cups cooked rice

2 cups chopped, cooked chicken

2 hard cooked eggs, peeled and chopped

1/2 cup chopped pimiento

1/2 cup chopped fresh parsley

Salt to taste

Cornstarch and water to thicken

In a large saucepan or kettle, combine water, onion, carrot, celery, green pepper, chicken base, white pepper and sugar; bring to boil, reduce heat, cover and simmer until vegetables are tender. Add rice, chicken, egg, pimiento and parsley. Season with salt and heat through, then thicken soup with cornstarch solution as desired. Yields 4 servings.

Source: Russ Waddle of Waddle's Restaurant in Portland.

Egg Salad Louie! Louie!

In a bowl, combine mayonnaise and chile sauce. Stir in eggs and celery and blend well. Yields 2 cups sandwich filling, enough for 6 to 8 regular-sized sandwiches.

EGG SALAD LOUIE! LOUIE!

1/2 cup mayonnaise

3 tablespoons commercial chile sauce

8 hard-cooked eggs, peeled and coarsely chopped

1/3 cup minced celery

Spinach Salad with 5-Minute Egg

This is a wonderful salad, but I've had mixed reviews. Know your diners' tastes. Some people are experimenters by nature, while others need a more gentle introduction to the world of artful salads. After trying this one out on the family, my husband waited until the dishes were cleared and children were out of earshot. Then he took me into his arms and sweetly whispered into my ear: "Don't ever serve that again."

Gently place eggs into a pan of simmering water and cook for exactly 5 minutes (do not let the water stop simmering). Remove from heat, drain carefully (don't crack eggs), then fill the pan with cold water and let the eggs cool completely. When cold, gently peel the eggs.

Place the spinach leaves in a large salad bowl, along with the olives and bacon. Toss with some of the vinaigrette, then arrange on six dinner plates. Place a handful of homemade croutons in the center of each salad. Place one of the eggs atop each bed of croutons, then drizzle a small amount of vinaigrette over each egg and sprinkle with Parmesan cheese. Yields 6 servings.

SPINACH SALAD WITH 5-MINUTE EGG

6 eggs, at room temperature

1 pound fresh spinach, washed, dried, tough stems removed, and broken into bite-sized pieces

1 cup pitted black olives

3 strips crisp-fried bacon, crumbled

Tarragon Vinaigrette (page 172)

Garlic Butter Croutons (page 162)

Grated Parmesan cheese

NOTE: To make sure you end up with beautifully peeled eggs, avoid just-purchased eggs. If eggs are extremely fresh, the white sometimes sticks to the shell when peeled.

Caesar Salad

It's still one of the best ways to wow a dinner crowd: splish, splash, mash, twirl and toss a Caesar salad that brings food sophisticates to their feet.

But a homemade Caesar salad is too often less than masterful. Not because it's such a complicated task. Come on! Parmesan cheese, olive oil, coddled egg, minced garlic, fresh lemon juice, a little Worcestershire and mashed anchovies? You'll find more complexity in a Wolfgang Puck cooking segment on Good Morning America.

No, the problem stems from the M-word. Mystique. Pseudo-gourmets have spent years building and reinforcing it, while gullible gourmands have bought into it. All too often this results in a cook reluctant to throw caution to the wind. The simple truth is that anyone armed with truly exquisite ingredients can make a delicious Caesar salad. And here's the good news for those not interested in showboating in front of a crowd: the act of twirling and tossing for the audience is strictly optional. Your masterpiece can be assembled in the privacy of your own kitchen or closet, and THEN brought to the table.

CAESAR SALAD

1 coddled egg (recipe follows)

1/4 cup fresh lemon juice

1 heaping tablespoon minced fresh garlic

1 tablespoon Dijon mustard

2 teaspoons Worcestershire sauce

Several dashes hot pepper sauce . . .

In a medium-sized bowl (or in the salad bowl if you're doing this at the dinner table), combine the egg, lemon juice, garlic, mustard, Worcestershire and hot pepper sauce. Whisk until well blended. Add the anchovy filets and mash into a paste with a fork. You can mash the anchovies separately and then add them to the lemon juice mixture, if you prefer. Slowly add olive oil, whisking well.

Salad can be prepared to this point up to 1 hour before

serving. Store in refrigerator. When ready to serve, add the lettuce leaves to the salad bowl and sprinkle generously with salt and freshly ground pepper. Toss with most of the dressing. Add the Parmesan and croutons and toss until all the lettuce and croutons are evenly coated with dressing, adding more dressing if necessary. Serve immediately. Yields 8 servings.

CODDLED EGG

To coddle an egg, first bring it to room temperature by running it under hot water for a moment (otherwise it might crack). Place it in a mug and pour boiling water over it; allow to stand for 1 minute.

Egg-Free Caesar Salad

Now for a bit of bad news. The United States Department of Agriculture has added the king of salads to its unsafe foods hit list. At fault is the practically raw egg, known to sometimes carry the accursed salmonella bacterium. They are targeting the information to high risk segments of the population: the elderly, very young, the pregnant, and those people who have been weakened by serious illness, or whose immune systems are weakened.

It's your kitchen and your call. If you prefer to leave the egg out, simply increase the olive oil to 1 cup, and add 1 scant tablespoon commercially made mayonnaise (homemade mayonnaise uses raw, unpasteurized eggs, which are what you're trying to avoid).

4 anchovy filets

3/4 cup extra virgin olive oil

1 large head romaine lettuce, washed, thoroughly dried, broken into 2- to 3-inch long pieces, and chilled

Salt and freshly ground black pepper

1 cup freshly shaved (somewhere between shredded and grated) Parmesan cheese

2 to 3 cups Garlic Butter Croutons (page 162)

Summer Gazpacho

Years ago I worked in a fine old hotel, the Ahwahnee, in Yosemite National Park. There, the chef made his own soup. From scratch, mind you, not cans, or even cans and fresh vegetables and cream. From scratch.

The process always began the evening before. Buckets of meat scraps, bones and vegetable cuttings were dumped into the hot-tub sized vat of water and left to bubble and simmer into a succulently rich broth.

By morning, once every molecule of flavor had been leached from the carrots, onions, celery and meat, Chef Roget would have them removed. Then he would make the soup.

Each mid-week day had its taste, depending on the season and weather. Some of my favorites included a velvety split pea with smoked ham, cream of tomato, a heavenly turkey noodle, and on most Fridays, a lobster bisque to die for. Saturday's menu featured two soups: a sparkling clear consommé and a vegetable bisque. Sundays were reserved for cream of chicken.

In the interest of variety and grande cuisine, Roget spent the greater part of each morning perfecting his soups. By noon, I would show up, spoon and bowl in hand. Roget considered me his official taste tester, not so much for my discerning palate as for my enthusiastic appreciation of his work.

The routine never varied. I would make my approach to the pot with a reconnaissance sniff, as though the possibility existed that I might choose not to sip. This was strictly for show, since Roget never made bad soup. After a moment's discussion over its character and color he would tip some into my bowl from his mammoth ladle.

The first few spoonsful were enjoyed near the pot so we could chat—usually about the guests I'd been dealing with that morning at the front desk, or a fiasco or two that may have occured in the dining room on the previous night.

By then the lunch orders would be coming in. Roget would have to return to his blazing stoves, so I would head outside into the crisp high Sierra air and find a comfortable crate on the loading dock. From that perch, with shimmering dogwoods and emerald pines for companionship, I would savor Roget's soup du jour to the last drop.

I didn't get any recipes out of Chef Roget before leaving Yosemite, but I learned something about good soup. This is one of my favorite Gazpacho creations. Feature it on a sultry summer evening when a light-but-spicy meal would hit the spot.

Combine all of the ingredients except garnishes in a large pot. Refrigerate for at least 8 hours, or overnight.

Serve very cold, with the garnishes alongside for diners to add at will. Yields 8 to 10 servings.

SUMMER GAZPACHO

3 large tomatoes, chopped

1 cucumber, peeled and chopped

1 green sweet bell pepper, seeded and chopped

1 bunch green onions, chopped

3 cups vegetable cocktail juice (such as V-8)

1 (10-1/2 ounce) can beef bouillon, undiluted

5 tablespoons wine vinegar

1/4 cup olive oil

1 cup mild salsa or picante sauce

2 teaspoons Worcestershire sauce . . .

1 teaspoon each: dried basil, dill

1/2 teaspoon salt

1/4 teaspoon hot pepper sauce

1 or 2 cloves garlic, crushed & minced

Garnishes: sour cream, fresh croutons,
*   avocado chunks, pickled jalapeño*
*   slices, tortilla chips, shredded cheese*

7-Grain Squaw Bread

The long-range weather forecast indicated that winter was moving in. With the first big snow Tioga Pass would be closed for the season—and along with it, opportunities to hike the east side of the Sierra Nevada just outside the boundaries of Yosemite National Park.

A group of us living and working in the park knew this was no time to second-guess the weather bureau. Backpacking gear and bodies were crammed into cars as we set out for a last visit to one of our favorite eastside trailheads: the base of Mammoth Mountain, just outside the tiny resort town of the same name.

It was the kind of October weekend that justifies the end of summer. Set against the crisp autumn-blue sky were the shimmering reds and golds of quaking aspen and vine maple. For the better part of two days we hiked our little hearts out, stopping only for sleep and light trail snacks. And so, by the time we made it back to the trailhead Sunday afternoon we were thinking more in terms of inhaling steaks than alpine ambience.

Unfortunately, once we reached town the five of us could barely scrape together six dollars and change. Supermarket fare would have to do. We picked out the heartiest looking loaf of bread in the store, a 7-grain variety called Squaw Bread, and a reasonable selection of cold cuts from the deli. Back out in the parking lot there ensued a frantic bout of sandwich construction on the hood of the car.

After that, silence, eventually giving way to muffled sighs and groans—the true indicators of a five-star meal. I've been partial to sandwiches for supper ever since.

With football games, school lunches and autumn picnics, you don't need a 22-mile hike to enjoy such portable fare. But a good 7-grain bread recipe might help.

In a medium saucepan, boil the 7-grain cereal with the water; reduce heat, cover and cook 8 minutes. Add honey, butter, salt and 1/2 to 3/4 cup additional 7-grain cereal to thicken. Cool to lukewarm (115° to 120°).

In a mixer bowl, combine whole wheat flour, yeast and instant non-fat dry milk. Add 7-grain mixture; beat at low speed 1/2 minute, scraping sides constantly. Beat 3 minutes at high speed. By hand, stir in enough white flour to make a medium-stiff dough. Turn onto floured surface. Knead 8 to 10 minutes. Shape into ball and place in greased bowl. Cover, and allow dough to rise in a warm place until it has doubled in size, 45 to 60 minutes.

Punch down dough; turn out onto floured surface. Divide dough in half; cover, and allow it to rest 10 minutes. Shape each half into a loaf. Place in greased 8- by 4- by 2-inch loaf pans or onto a greased baking sheet. Cover, allow loaves to rise in warm place until their size has doubled (30 minutes). Bake in 400° oven for 30 to 35 minutes.

7-GRAIN SQUAW BREAD

1 cup 7-grain cereal

3-1/4 cups water

1/3 cup honey

3 tablespoons butter

2 teaspoons salt

2 cups whole wheat flour

2 packages yeast

1/3 cup instant non-fat dry milk

4-1/2 cups white flour

Source: a friend, Sylvia Stewart, many years ago.

Garlic Butter Croutons

After a full day of hiking in the Sierras, a group of us descended upon our favorite high country eatery, The June Lake Inn. After taking our orders, the waitress brought back frosty beers and a bowl of homemade croutons for munching. The croutons didn't have a chance—they were gone in three minutes. Two bowls later we were sated for the night, but not for life. Here's my version.

GARLIC BUTTER CROUTONS

4 – 6 sourdough English muffins
1/3 cup melted butter
2 teaspoons Worcestershire sauce
1/2 teaspoon minced garlic
1/2 teaspoon dry mustard
1/4 teaspoon salt

Split the muffins in half and cut into 3/4-inch cubes; spread the cubes on a baking sheet.

In a small cup, combine the butter, Worcestershire sauce, garlic, mustard and salt. With a spoon, drizzle the butter mixture over the cubes of bread, making sure that each cube gets a healthy dose.

Bake in a 375° oven for about 10 minutes, or until croutons are golden and slightly crunchy. Yields about 4 cups.

Unused croutons can be stored in a closed plastic bag up to several days, or frozen.

Mrs. Duncan's Drop Scones

Consider the scone: it's always amazed me how one little tea cake with such a short name can have so many variations—both in preparation and pronunciation. There are griddle scones and oven scones, baking-soda scones and yeast scones, treacle scones and sweet cream scones. As far as pronunciation is concerned, our family says scone so that it rhymes with "on." But it's just as often pronounced with a long "o"—and in some parts of Scotland, the word has acquired an extra syllable, yielding "scoo-en".

At Scottish banquets, I'd sample other people's scones. Some were extremely fluffy and contained moist raisins; others were made from treacle. There was even one that Margaret Jack always brought that didn't resemble a scone at all. It reminded me of plain old pancakes, except it had a velvety smooth surface, and inside, it was spongy, not doughy or cakey.

I liked Margaret's funny little pancake scones, but as a child, it never occurred to me to obtain the recipe. In college, long after Mrs. Jack's demise, I set out to duplicate her scone. I finally found a likely candidate in one of my Scottish cookbooks. It was called Mrs. Duncan's Drop Scones, and it came pretty close. Even my roommates appreciated their unusual texture and slightly sweet flavor, so we'd make up huge batches and store them in the freezer for midnight study breaks.

Mix the dry ingredients in a bowl. With a wire whip, stir in egg and buttermilk. Pour batter in 3-inch rounds on a medium-hot, lightly greased griddle.

Cook scones until they are lightly browned on underside and covered with small bubbles on top. Turn and cook other side. Place in a folded tea towel until ready to serve. Serve hot or cold, with butter and strawberry jam, lemon curd, or honey. Yields 12 scones.

MRS. DUNCAN'S DROP SCONES

2 cups flour

1/2 teaspoon salt

2 tablespoons sugar

1-1/2 teaspoons baking powder

1/4 teaspoon baking soda

1 egg

1-3/4 cup buttermilk

Oregon Big Cheese Muffins

My first professional job out of college was in a San Francisco free-lance test kitchen. During my initial interview, the owner probed me about my cooking skills.

"What kind of cooking experience have you had?" she asked.

I explained my technical background in college, adding that "Actually, I've been cooking since I could reach the kitchen counter with the aid of a chair."

"But can you REALLY cook," she thundered. "Can you just walk into the kitchen—without the aid of a cookbook—and mix up a batch of...muffins?"

"Of course I can."

"Good," she said. "Then tomorrow, for our second interview, why don't you just whip up a few things for me in the kitchen."

I went home and read all about muffins.

OREGON BIG CHEESE MUFFINS

*1 cup white or unbleached all-purpose
   flour*

1 cup whole wheat flour

2 teaspoons baking powder

1/2 teaspoon baking soda

1/2 teaspoon salt

1/8 teaspoon ground black pepper

1-1/2 cups extra sharp Cheddar cheese

1 cup plain lowfat yogurt

1/2 cup milk

1 egg, beaten

3 tablespoons butter, melted

Butter 12 muffin pan cups (1/3 cup capacity each) or 48 miniatures (2 tablespoons capacity each), making sure to butter around top of each. In a medium bowl, combine all-purpose and whole wheat flours, baking powder, baking soda, salt and pepper; mix well. Add 1 cup of the cheese. In a small bowl combine yogurt, milk, egg and butter; mix well. Add all at once to dry ingredients. Stir with a fork just until dry ingredients are moistened. DO NOT OVERMIX. Spoon into prepared pans, then sprinkle with remaining 1/2 cup cheese. Bake in a 375° oven until tops are golden, 20 to 25 minutes for large muffins, or 12 minutes for miniatures. Carefully remove from pans.

Source: The Oregon Dairy Council.

Oregon Bleu Cheese Bread

At the Ark Restaurant on Washington State's Long-beach Peninsula, the aroma of Chef Main's freshly baked breads greets guests as they arrive. Oregon Bleu Cheese Bread is one of her most special creations. Roquefort or other blue-veined cheese will do in place of Oregon Bleu. However, the Ark uses only Oregon Bleu, of course.

Dissolve the yeast in the warm water. Stir in 2 table-spoons of the sugar and 1-1/2 cups of the flour until smooth. Allow this to sit until it bubbles, about 20 minutes.

Meanwhile, scald the milk (page 97) and pour it over a mixture of the salt, butter and dried onions, and the remaining 2 tablespoons of sugar. Let mixture cool to lukewarm, and then add it to the sponge (the yeast mixture). Add the egg(s) and Worcestershire.

Stir in 5 to 6 cups of the flour, the bleu cheese and the chopped chives. Empty dough onto a bed of 1 cup flour and knead until smooth (10 to 15 minutes). Put dough in greased bowl and invert to oil top. Cover bowl with plastic wrap, place in warm area away from drafts and allow dough to rise for an hour. Punch down and form into 3 loaves; put into greased pans or put 3 round loaves on flat pans. Alternatively, the recipe makes about 45 dinner rolls.

Allow dough to rise for 45 minutes, covered. Ten minutes before baking, score tops. Brush with milk and bake in 350° oven for 35 to 45 minutes (25 minutes for rolls). Right after removing bread from oven, brush tops with egg wash (1 beaten egg added to 1 tablespoon water) for gloss.

You'll love eating this bread fresh and warm with sweet butter. But you can also use it for appetizers, toast it, or

OREGON BLEU CHEESE BREAD

2 ounces yeast

1-1/2 cups warm water (115 to 120°)

4 tablespoons sugar

About 8-1/2 cups unbleached white flour

1 cup milk

1 tablespoon salt

3 tablespoons butter

2 tablespoons dried onions

1 or 2 eggs

1 teaspoon Worcestershire sauce

*2 ounces coarsely crumbled Oregon
   Bleu cheese*

1 tablespoon chopped chives

make sandwiches. Treat yourself to a real surprise: try a grilled cheese sandwich with Havarti cheese on Bleu Cheese Bread.

Source: *The Ark. Cuisine of the Pacific Northwest,* by Jimella Lucas and Nanci Main, Ladysmith Ltd. Publishers.

Curry Vinaigrette Dressing

CURRY VINAIGRETTE DRESSING

1/2 cup white wine vinegar

2 tablespoons fresh chives, minced

1 tablespoon curry powder

2 teaspoons packed light brown sugar

1 teaspoon soy sauce

1 clove garlic, minced

1/2 cup virgin olive oil

Combine the vinegar, chives, curry powder, sugar, soy sauce, and garlic and blend well. Whip in the oil until well blended. Yields about 1 cup dressing.

Fresh Spinach Presto Sauce

I had been working with spinach and had come up with a lovely sauce that was quite pesto-like in appearance, yet delicately flavored with sautéed onions, garlic, and just a hint of basil.

As much as I love a fine, classic pesto, my husband finds it about as subtle as a jackhammer. Neither he nor my eldest son knew that the green sauce awaiting them on a bed of fettuccini was made from spinach instead of basil. "I don't DO pesto," announced The Light-Of-My-Life. The seventeen-year-old nodded his support.

"Well, my PETS," I responded in a metered, don't-tread-on-me, tone, "this isn't pesto, it's spinach. So shut your eyes and pretend it's a lah-dee-dah Onion Florentine Sauce. I think you'll be pleasantly surprised."

They did, and they were, so the meal was a success after all. The remainder of the sauce was sealed up and refrigerated. But instead of using it to work out some planned spin-off recipes, I found myself dipping into it serendipitously throughout the week. One night I placed dollops of it atop of our grilled chicken breasts. Another time it became the basis for a quick pasta salad. It even worked as a sandwich spread with sun-dried tomatoes, Swiss cheese, and pickled Greek pepperoncini. Try it as an accent for pork chops or fish filets too.

This is a delectable, speedy, make-ahead sauce. Refrigerated, it maintains good color and flavor for at least a week. It could probably go longer, but I haven't managed to leave a batch alone long enough to be sure.

Sauté the onion and garlic in about 4 tablespoons of the olive oil until onion is soft and transparent; remove from heat and cool slightly. Spoon the onion and oil mixture into a blender or food processor. Add spinach, basil and salt. Process until mixture is finely chopped. With motor running, pour the remaining 1/4 cup of olive oil in a slow but steady stream through the feeder hole. Blend to a coarse purée, then stop the motor, add cheese and process for just a moment more. Yields 1-1/4 cups sauce.

FRESH SPINACH PRESTO SAUCE

1 cup chopped yellow onion

1/2 cup olive oil, divided

3 cloves garlic, peeled and minced

3 cups fresh spinach leaves, firmly packed

2 teaspoons dried basil

1/2 teaspoon salt

1/4 cup Parmesan cheese (preferably freshly grated)

Duxelles

Nothing takes the place of this succulently rich pâté of finely minced mushrooms and shallots sautéed in butter and Madeira wine. Duxelles (pronounced "du-sell") is absolutely divine spread on rounds of Melba toast—or any other plain cracker that won't overpower the delicate flavors. The nice thing is that duxelles is the perfect answer for those tired out mushrooms that are still good but too homely to use when appearance counts.

Melt butter in a large, deep skillet. Add mushrooms, shallots and onion and sauté over medium-high heat, stirring frequently. After several minutes, the mushrooms will release their liquid. Continue cooking, until the mixture becomes quite dry and darker in color. Add salt, pepper and sherry. Continue cooking over medium-high heat until mixture thickens again. Refrigerate until ready to use. Yields 2 cups.

Duxelles is something to have on hand at all times; it stores in the refrigerator for up to 2 weeks, and in the freezer for up to 3 months.

DUXELLES

1/2 cup butter

1 pound mushrooms, finely minced (a food processor works best)

2 shallots, finely minced (mince the shallots in the food processor with the mushrooms)

2 tablespoons finely minced onion

1/2 teaspoon salt

1/4 teaspoon white pepper

1/3 cup dry sherry or Madeira

Raita Sauce

Combine all of the ingredients in a small bowl; adjust seasonings. Chill for at least 1 hour before serving to allow flavors to blend. Yields scant 2-3/4 cups.

RAITA SAUCE

1 cucumber, peeled, seeded and chopped

1/2 cup finely chopped yellow onion

1 cup plain yogurt

1 cup sour cream

1 to 2 teaspoons cumin powder

Salt and pepper to taste

Guacamole

Place all of the ingredients in blender or food processor and blend to desired consistency (completely smooth, or with some lumps still remaining). Adjust seasonings. Refrigerate up to 3 hours before needed. Yields about 2 cups.

GUACAMOLE

3 ripe avocados (preferably Hass),
    peeled, seeded, and quartered

1/4 cup mayonnaise

1/2 tomato, coarsely chopped

2 tablespoons green taco sauce

1 tablespoon fresh lemon juice

1 teaspoon Worcestershire sauce

1 teaspoon chopped cilantro

1/2 teaspoon salt (more or less to taste)

Pocket Delight Vinaigrette

In a small, deep bowl, combine the vinegar, Worcestershire, salt, cumin, pepper, and pepper sauce; beat with wire whisk to blend. Continue beating while adding the olive and salad oils. Finally, stir in sour cream and blend again. Chill for at least 1 hour before serving. Yields 1-1/8 cups.

POCKET DELIGHT VINAIGRETTE

1/3 cup wine vinegar

2 teaspoons Worcestershire sauce

1/2 teaspoon salt

1 teaspoon cumin powder

1/4 teaspoon white pepper

1/8 teaspoon hot pepper sauce (such as
    Tabasco)

1/4 cup extra virgin olive oil

1/4 cup salad oil

1/3 cup sour cream

Sesame & Poppy Seed Vinaigrette

There is no bacon in this dressing, but the combination of toasted sesame and poppy seeds makes it seem as though there is. Because of its bacon-like flavor, this dressing is particularly wonderful on a spinach salad tossed with toasted almonds, fresh tomato chunks and slivers of a really good Swiss cheese.

SESAME & POPPY SEED
  VINAIGRETTE

4 tablespoons wine vinegar

1 tablespoon sugar

2 tablespoons lightly toasted sesame
  seeds

1 tablespoon poppy seeds

1 tablespoon coarsely chopped onion

1/2 teaspoon Worcestershire sauce

1/4 teaspoon paprika

1/4 to 1/2 teaspoon salt

1/3 cup vegetable oil

Place the vinegar, salt, sesame seeds, poppy seeds, onion, Worcestershire, paprika and salt into blender or food processor. Blend until most of the sesame seeds are ground (stop the motor several times and scrape down the sides of the container). With a rubber spatula, scrape the contents into a small bowl; whisk in the vegetable oil. Yields about 3/4 cup.

CREAMY VERSION

After blending all of the ingredients (except the oil) as described previously, keep the motor running and add the oil in a slow, steady stream. The dressing will thicken up to the consistency of a soft homemade mayonnaise. If you prefer the creamy version, do not toss it with the greens. Instead, lay a dollop of it on each individual serving, and pass the rest in a bowl.

Spiced German Mustard

We'd been in Paris less than four hours and were wandering along the Left Bank when hunger struck. Although a traditional French bistro was high on our itinerary, my friends and I agreed that the sausage vendor's cart less than 10 yards away had lunch written all over it. The delicious aroma wafting its way noseward was irresistible.

After tucking the plump and juicy sausages into steamy-hot and crusty rolls, the vendor waggled her finger between two mustard pots.

"Spicy or no?" she asked.

"Spicy!" we said in unison, and she slathered our picnic fare with a deep golden condiment flecked with tiny yellow and brown mustard seeds.

We crossed the road to the river and settled ourselves on top of a huge stone wall, the Seine passing just 20 feet below our dangling Nikes. There, with Paris all around, I took my first bite of my first French meal—and vowed that when I returned to the states I would track down this fantastic mustard and stock vast amounts of it in my refrigerator.

Well, not only did I become an avid buyer of the varied styles and types of mustard, I also learned how to produce that zesty wonder in my own kitchen. You can, too. Making mustard is a snap.

This recipe for Spiced German Mustard is as close as you can come to the commercially-made product I fell in love with years ago over the Seine. It's a simple concoction to throw together, and it stores nicely in the refrigerator.

Your best chance for locating yellow, brown and black mustard seeds is a store where a large variety of bulk spices are sold. Don't make mustard using the tiny jars you buy in the spice section of the supermarket. The cost would be prohibitive.

Better to put those precious pennies toward a trip to Paris. I know a terrific sausage vendor on the West Bank.

SPICED GERMAN MUSTARD

1/3 cup mustard seeds (a blending of
   1/4 cup yellow and a heaping 2 tablespoons of black or brown is a good
   mix. If you can't obtain the black or
   brown, use the yellow alone)

1/4 cup powdered mustard

1/2 cup cold water

1 cup cider vinegar

1 small onion, chopped

2 tablespoons firmly packed brown
   sugar

1 teaspoon salt

2 garlic cloves, minced or pressed

1/2 teaspoon cinnamon

1/4 teaspoon each: ground allspice, dill
   seed, dry tarragon leaves

1/8 teaspoon turmeric

In a small bowl, combine mustard seeds, powdered mustard and water. Stir thoroughly to blend; soak for at least 3 hours.

In a 1- to 2-quart non-aluminum pan, combine vinegar, onion, sugar, salt, garlic and spices. Simmer, uncovered, on medium heat until reduced by half, 10 to 15 minutes. Pour the vinegar mixture through a wire strainer into the mustard mixture. Whirl in a blender until puréed to the texture you like. An authentic German mustard will have quite a few whole seeds remaining. Cook in upper pan of a double boiler, stirring occasionally, until thickened, 10 to 15 minutes.

Cool, then cover and age at least three days in the refrigerator. Mustard will keep refrigerated for 2 years. Yields about 1 cup. Recipe can easily be doubled or tripled.

Source: *Gift Ideas From the Kitchen,* compiled by Oregon State University Extension Master Food Preservers.

Tarragon Vinaigrette

TARRAGON VINAIGRETTE

1 tablespoon Dijon mustard

1 egg yolk

3 tablespoons red or white wine vinegar

1/2 teaspoon salt

1/4 teaspoon dried tarragon

1/8 teaspoon powdered savory

1/8 teaspoon white pepper

3/4 cup salad oil (equal parts of extra –
   virgin olive and safflower oils)

In a small bowl, combine the mustard, egg yolk, vinegar, salt, tarragon, savory and pepper; blend well with a wire whisk. Add the oils in a slow stream, whisking constantly, until the dressing is thick and blended. Adjust seasonings and set the dressing aside. If you make the dressing more than 30 minutes ahead of time, refrigerate until ready to use. Yields 1-1/4 cups.

Teriyaki Sauce

Combine all ingredients in small bowl or jar. Sauce will keep in the refrigerator for up to 1 month. Yields about 2 cups.

TERIYAKI SAUCE

1 cup soy sauce

1/2 cup dry sherry

1/2 cup firmly packed brown sugar

1/4 cup fresh lemon juice

3 to 4 cloves garlic, finely minced or pressed

2 teaspoons Chinese mustard

2 teaspoons finely minced fresh ginger

Hazelnut Wafers with Raspberries & Chocolate

The life of a foodwriter is not one big bowl of cherries. At times, there's plenty of rutabaga and squash. That also applies from my family's point of view—literally. When I'm developing recipes for edibles that are, shall we say, not from the mainstream, the normal stampede to the dinner table definitely calms into more of a coy sashay.

Just ask my youngest son. During any given week, he may have to dodge more spinach, beets or eggplant than most kids see in an entire school term.

How does he handle it? He eats carrots.

And then there's our oldest son. The Trooper. He's stiff-upper-lipped his way through some unusual experiments. Recipes that will never stain a page. But even for him, there's a limit. "I have an idea," he said once, gently nudging a greenish-grey mass of tomatillo casserole aside with his fork. "Maybe you should do an article on 'How To Avoid Disasters In The Kitchen.' "

So one Valentine's Day I decided to create something extra special in their honor. Something decadently delicious, for sure, but also beautiful to behold. An offering of love. Sweets for my sweeties.

This is what I came up with.

HAZELNUT WAFERS WITH
RASPBERRIES & CHOCOLATE

3/4 cup butter, at room temperature
3/4 cup sugar
1-1/3 cups all-purpose flour
1 cup of whole hazelnuts, toasted,
  rubbed between your palms to remove
  skins, and finely chopped
Raspberry jam (preferably a good
  quality Oregon variety)
5 or 6 ounces of a good quality semi-
  sweet chocolate (such as Lindt's),
  melted

Cream together butter and sugar with an electric mixer until light and fluffy. Stir in flour and hazelnuts (dough will seem grainy). Roll out the dough on a lightly floured surface to 1/8- to 1/4-inch thickness. Cut into rounds using a 2-inch cookie cutter. Using a spatula, transfer the rounds to greased cookie sheets. Bake in the upper third of a 375° oven for about 9 minutes, just until wafers begin to brown around the edges. Wafers should cool for at least 10 minutes before being moved to a wire rack (or cool completely on the baking sheet). When cool, place a 1/2-inch dollop of jam in the center of each wafer. Spread the jam out to a diameter of about 1 inch. Fill a pastry bag, or a small resealable plastic bag with a tiny hole cut in the corner, with the melted chocolate. Drizzle the chocolate in a lacy pattern on each cookie. The chocolate will firm up in about 10 minutes. Makes 40 cookies.

Frozen Strawberry Daiquiri Mix

FROZEN STRAWBERRY DAIQUIRI MIX

2 cups granulated sugar
1/3 cup lime juice (juice from 2 medium
  limes)
1/4 cup water
1 quart fresh strawberries, washed and
  hulled

Combine sugar, lime juice and water in a bowl. Stir to mix, and then let stand until sugar is almost completely dissolved, about 15 minutes (mixture will be thick).

In a blender or food processor, combine the sugar and lime juice with the berries. Blend until smooth, pack into freezer containers, and freeze. The mixture will harden to the consistency of a very firm sherbet, so you will be able to scoop portions from the main batch, then reseal its container. An alternative method for packing would be to pour the mixture into ice cube trays and freeze until firm, then unmold and pack into resealable freezer bags. Yields about 4-2/3 cups.

For each strawberry daiquiri: In blender jar, combine 3 tablespoons rum (light or dark), 1/4 cup Frozen Strawberry Daiquiri Mix (2 average-sized cubes that have been frozen in ice cube trays) and about 3/4 cup of ice cubes (7 or 8 average sized cubes). Blend until smooth. Most blender jars can handle up to 4 servings.

For a non-alcoholic frozen drink, replace the rum with unsweetened pineapple juice.

For a Strawberry Piña Colada: In blender jar, combine 3 tablespoons rum (light or dark), 1/4 cup Frozen Strawberry Daiquiri Mix, 3 tablespoons unsweetened pineapple juice, 1 tablespoon coconut cream, and about 3/4 cup of ice cubes. For a non-alcoholic version, omit the rum.

Summer Blackberry Pie

To a 10-year-old fresh from battle with a blackberry bush, there's no greater taste of victory than blackberry pie.

I still feel that way. And I'm not even what you'd call a pie person—usually. But when the heady, almost cloying fragrance of sunbaked berries hits the summer air, I know it's time to dust off the rolling pin, pry the pastry blender from the depths of my gadget drawer and lay in a fresh supply of Crisco.

I know all the emotional hurdles encountered by people who don't do pastry. But when you get desperate for a berry pie, you work through those misgivings. I'll bet you've got stacks of laundry that take longer to do than a berry pie. If you can just keep the procedure in that perspective, you should be rolling and crimping in no time.

SUMMER BLACKBERRY PIE

Pastry for 2-crust pie (recipe follows)
1 to 1-1/2 cups sugar
1/3 cup flour
4 heaping cups fresh blackberries, (or raspberries, loganberries, or Marionberries)
2 tablespoons butter or margarine
1 egg white, lightly beaten

Fit bottom crust into the pie pan. Combine sugar and flour; set aside. Place the berries in pastry-lined pie pan, alternating layers with the sugar/flour mixture. Don't be afraid of piling too high, because the filling really cooks down flat if you don't. They should mound nicely. Dot surface with butter.

Fit top crust over berries; flute edges decoratively and cut vents. Paint the upper crust with lightly beaten egg white. Then decorate with pieces of pastry (cut in shapes such as leaves or flowers) if desired, and brush the decoration with additional egg white. Sprinkle with granulated sugar. Bake in 425° oven for 35 to 40 minutes, or until crust is golden. Yields one 9-inch pie.

PASTRY FOR 2-CRUST PIE

2 cups flour
1 teaspoon salt
3/4 cup vegetable shortening
5 tablespoons cold water

Combine flour and salt in mixing bowl. With pastry blender, cut in vegetable shortening until flour is just blended to form pea-sized chunks. Sprinkle water, one tablespoon at a time, into the flour mixture, tossing lightly with a fork until dough will form a ball. Divide dough into 2 parts. Press each piece between hands to form two 5- to 6-inch rounds.

Roll out each round on a floured surface, using a floured rolling pin. For bottom crust, trim the circle of dough to 1 inch larger than the 9-inch pie plate.

Grandma Skinner's Scottish Shortbread

I can still remember her hands—those strong, lined hands of my grandmother's, delicately tapered at the fingertips, working their way through a bowl of dough.

With each December came her holiday gift preparations, and I was her indefatigable helper. I measured out dusty cups of flour for the Scottish Shortbread, and kept an eagle eye on the oven as the rounds were magically transformed from pale raw dough to lightly golden rounds.

There was nothing unique about the recipe—just flour, sugar and butter, in decadently rich proportions. She thoroughly blended the ingredients with her hands. No spoon, wooden or otherwise, could work as efficiently, nor offer the warmth to soften the butter properly as it was creamed into the sugar. Then she pressed the dough into a beautiful old wooden shortbread mold.

The mold, about 8 inches in diameter and 3/4 inch deep, was hand-carved by my great-grandfather in Scotland. The center design, a dramatic, large thistle with two spiky leaves, was surrounded by an accordion-like spiral border. One batch of dough was exactly right for two rounds of shortbread.

After decades of use, the mold was well-seasoned. A light dusting of flour was the only preparation necessary before Grandma gently pressed the dough onto its surface. I would watch her give the treasured sculpture a few well-placed taps against the counter, then invert it over a paper-lined cookie sheet so the dough could obediently descend from its face.

GRANDMA SKINNER'S SCOTTISH
SHORTBREAD

2-1/2 cups white flour

1/2 cup granulated sugar

1 cup butter, softened to room temperature

Cream together butter and sugar, preferably using your hands. Gradually mix in the flour, kneading the dough until all of the flour is combined and mixture is smooth.

Place the dough in an ungreased 8-inch round cake pan. Pat down and prick all over with a fork. Bake in 325° oven until golden brown, 20 to 25 minutes. While still warm, cut the round into desired number of wedges.

Index

Index